ELEMENTARY

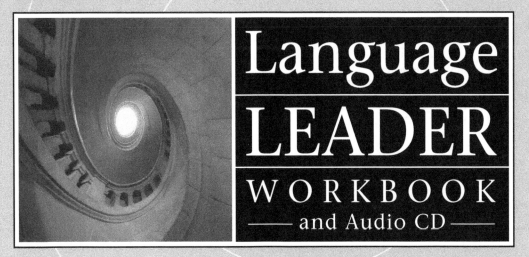

Language
LEADER
WORKBOOK
and Audio CD

D'Arcy Adrian-Vallance

CONTENTS

LANGUAGE LEADER **ELEMENTARY**

CONTENTS

Listening	Spelling / Pronunciation	Scenario	Study & Writing skills
Cities, population, international telephone codes DICTATION	Spelling: vowel groups	Key language: Saying where places are	Using your dictionary (1) A description of a city TRANSLATION
Jobs: places and feelings LISTEN BETTER: Listen and understand DICTATION	Spelling: Words with –tion Pronunciation: s endings	Key language: Asking for information (1)	Using your dictionary (2) An application form TRANSLATION
A lecture DICTATION	Spelling and Pronunciation: Silent letters	Key language: Making suggestions	Classroom language Description of a process TRANSLATION
Choosing a film LISTEN BETTER : Listening for stressed words DICTATION	Spelling: -er or -or Pronunciation: /ð/	Key language: Asking for information (2), saying no politely	Working with numbers: large numbers, fractions, percentages A description of a pie chart TRANSLATION
Radio programme – people's preferences DICTATION	Spelling: e, ee and ea Pronunciation: Vowel sounds	Key language: Buying a ticket	Planning your written work TRANSLATION
Description LISTEN BETTER : Guessing DICTATION	Spelling: Double and single consonants, e, ee and ea Pronunciation: Sounds and word stress	Key language: Requests and offers	Correcting your writing A restaurant review TRANSLATION
Shopping conversations DICTATION	Spelling: Adding -ing Pronunciation: Stressed words	Key language: Giving advantages and disadvantages	Giving a short, informal talk An informal email TRANSLATION
A talk on Roman civilisation LISTEN BETTER – Signposts in listening DICTATION	Spelling: Similar words Pronunciation: /tʃ/, /k/, /ʃ/	Key language: Polite requests	Learning new words A description of an object TRANSLATION
Talk on inventors and their inventions DICTATION	Spelling: Long words Pronunciation: Stressed syllables	Key language: Giving reasons	Taking notes Short biographies TRANSLATION
A conversation LISTEN BETTER : Main ideas and details DICTATION	Spelling: ant, ent, int Pronunciation: Diphthongs, Stressed words	Key language: Asking for and giving opinions	A formal letter TRANSLATION
A talk on predictions in the past DICTATION	Spelling: One word or two? Pronunciation: Stessed words	Key language: Checking understanding	Examination skills An informal letter TRANSLATION
A radio programme LISTEN BETTER : Preparation for listening DICTATION	Spelling: Some problem words Pronunciation: British places	Key language:Giving a short talk	Learning outside classroom Titles and addresses TRANSLATION

1 Cities

1.1 CITY FACTS

VOCABULARY: adjectives

1 Choose the best word, a), b) or c), to complete the sentences.

1 It's hot and _dry_ .
   a) wet   b) noisy   c) dry

2 It's cold and _____.
   a) hot   b) wet   c) new

3 It's a _____ restaurant.
   a) cheap   b) big   c) quiet

4 It's _____.
   a) ugly   b) small   c) beautiful

5 It's _____.
   a) old   b) good   c) small

6 It's _____.
   a) bad   b) quiet   c) wet

7 It's a _____ English football club.
   a) famous   b) expensive
   c) cold

EXTRA VOCABULARY: months, seasons

2 [2] Listen and repeat the months.

1 January	5 May	9 September
2 February	6 June	10 October
3 March	7 July	11 November
4 April	8 August	12 December

3 Which months are in which seasons in *your* country? Write the months under the seasons.

Spring	Summer

Autumn	Winter

4 Complete the sentences about your country. Write months or seasons in the blanks.

1 It's beautiful in _____ and _____.
2 It's hot in _____.
3 It's cold in _____.
4 It's wet in _____.
5 It's dry in _____.

SPELLING: vowel groups

5 Write one word from this page on each line.

ea   _cheap_ _____

_____

ou   _about_ _____

_____

oo   _____

_____

au   _____

_____

GRAMMAR: *to be*

6 Read the text about Amsterdam. Choose the correct word.

Amsterdam ¹is/are the capital of Holland.
²It/They is a beautiful city. It ³is/are cold in winter but warm in summer.

Dan, Bob and Ana ⁴is/are students. ⁵They/She are at a café in Amsterdam. Dan and Bob ⁶they/are English, but Ana is ⁷no/not.

7a Complete the conversation between Ana, Bob and Dan.

ANA: ¹ *Are* you from London?

BOB: No, we ²_____. I'm from Oxford, and Dan ³_____ from Manchester.

ANA: Oxford and Manchester ⁴_____ famous cities.

DAN: Are ⁵_____?

ANA: Yes, they are! Oxford University ⁶_____ famous, and Manchester United football club ⁷_____ famous.

DAN: I'm in a football club in Manchester, but it ⁸_____ the famous club!

ANA: Are ⁹_____ footballers?

DAN: No, we aren't. ¹⁰_____ students at Manchester University. ¹¹_____ *you* a student?

ANA: Yes, I ¹²_____.

BOB: ¹³_____ ¹⁴_____ from the USA?

ANA: No, ¹⁵_____ ¹⁶_____. I'm from Vancouver in Canada.

DAN: ¹⁷_____ Vancouver in the west of Canada?

ANA: Yes, it is. ¹⁸_____ a beautiful city.

7b 3 Listen and check your answers.

8 4 Listen to the questions. Choose the correct answer.

1 ~~No, I'm not.~~ / No, it isn't.

2 Yes, I am. / Yes, it is.

3 Yes, they are. / Yes, he is.

4 No, she isn't. / No, he isn't.

5 Yes, he is. / Yes, it is.

6 Yes, it is. / Yes, they are.

7 No, it isn't. / No, he isn't.

TRANSLATION

9 Translate into your language. Notice the differences.

1 Are you a student? Yes, I am.

_____

2 Is it a cheap restaurant? No, it isn't.

_____

3 The restaurants are not expensive.

_____

4 She is English.

_____

VOCABULARY: places in a city

1 Read the descriptions and complete the words.

1 a building for films   c <u>i</u> n <u>e</u> m <u>a</u>

2 a place for boats   h _ _ _ _ _ _

3 There are a lot in Venice.   c _ _ _ _ _

4 a big building with old things in it   m _ _ _ _ _

2 Choose the best word, a), b) or c), to complete the sentences.

1 There's a big _fountain_ in the park.
   a) fountain   b) city   c) airport

2 There are a lot of _____ on the beach.
   a) mountains   b) cinemas   c) boats

3 A lot of _____ are beautiful buildings.
   a) cities   b) temples   c) parks

4 There are 12 bridges in the _____.
   a) church   b) city   c) theatre

5 This is a famous _____ in San Francisco.
   a) bridge   b) airport   c) theatre

3 Add words to the _ea_ and _ou_ spelling lists in Exercise 5 on page 6.

EXTRA VOCABULARY: numbers

4 5 Listen and learn the numbers.

0 zero / oh / nought	10 ten	20 twenty
1 one	11 eleven	21 twenty-one
2 two	12 twelve	22 twenty-two
3 three	13 thirteen	23 twenty-three
4 four	14 fourteen	
5 five	15 fifteen	
6 six	16 sixteen	
7 seven	17 seventeen	
8 eight	18 eighteen	
9 nine	19 nineteen	

LISTENING

5 6 Listen and complete the tables.

Population		
1	Moscow, Russia	_14 million_
2	London, UK	
3	Istanbul, Turkey	
4	Paris, France	

International telephone codes		
1	Moscow	_795_
2	London	
3	Istanbul	
4	Paris	

GRAMMAR: there is, there are

6 Make sentences about Moscow. Match 1–6 with a–f.

1 There is a   a) any beaches?

2 There are   b) any beaches.

3 There isn't   c) five airports.

4 There aren't   d) an airport?

5 Is there   e) famous opera house.

6 Are there   f) a harbour.

7 Complete the sentences.

1 _There are_ about 14 million people in Moscow.

2 Q: _____ a lot of museums in Moscow?
   A: Yes. _____ 141 museums in Moscow.

3 Q: _____ a harbour in Paris?
   A: No, _____. Paris isn't near the sea.

4 _____ 143 parks in London.

5 Q: _____ a university in Istanbul?
   A: Yes. _____ 13 universities in Istanbul.

6 _____ a very famous museum in Paris – the Louvre.

7 _____ any mountains in Holland.

READING

8a Read about the city of Tallinn in Estonia.

Estonia is a small country in northern Europe between Russia and Finland. Tallinn is the capital city. It is a modern city, but in the old centre there are beautiful buildings from the 1200s. In this part of the city, a lot of the streets are very small, so there aren't any cars on them. There are good restaurants and cafés, and they aren't expensive. There are beautiful parks, interesting museums and three beaches, too.

The weather is good in summer, but not very hot. In July it is about 20°C. In winter, it is cold and often below zero.

There is an airport 4 kilometres from the city centre, and there are good buses from the airport to the city.

8b Are the sentences about Tallinn true or false?

1 Tallinn is the capital of Estonia. *true*

2 The centre of the city is new.

3 There are a lot of cars in the old part of the city.

4 The cafés and restaurants in Tallinn are expensive.

5 There are seven beaches.

6 The winters are cold, but the summers are not.

7 There is an airport in the city centre.

READ BETTER

Do you read from word to word?

👁 👁

Estonia → is → a → small → country → in → northern → Europe

Read from chunk to chunk. It's better.

👁 👁

Estonia is → a small country → in northern Europe

WRITING

9 Rewrite the 'false' sentences from Exercise 8. Make them true.

1 *(2) The centre of the city is old.*

2 _____

3 _____

4 _____

5 _____

1 Write seven places in a city. Use words from the box on the left and the box on the right. You can use the words in the box on the right more than once.

bus car information post railway shopping swimming	centre office park pool station stop

1 _bus stop_

2 _____

3 _____

4 _____

5 _____

6 _____

7 _____

2 Complete the labels with the correct prepositions.

1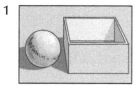

next to

2

_____

3

_____

4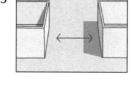

_____

3a Complete the phone conversation with the words in the box.

and between I'm in is isn't on opposite right there there's

MARIA: Hi Ellie, it's Maria.

ELLIE: Hi Maria. I'm ¹ _in_ the market. Are you in the bus station?

MARIA: Yes, I am.

ELLIE: Is ² _____ a café in the bus station?

MARIA: Yes, there is, but it ³ _____ very good. Is there a café in the market?

ELLIE: No, but ⁴ _____ a good café in South Street. It's ⁵ _____ the market and the bus station.

MARIA: Is it the street ⁶ _____ the bus station?

ELLIE: Yes, it ⁷ _____.

MARIA: OK. Is the café ⁸ _____ the left or the right?

ELLIE: It's on the ⁹ _____. It's between the post office ¹⁰ _____ the tourist information centre.

MARIA: OK. See you there in 5 minutes.

3b 〔7〕 Listen and check your answers.

4 Where are *you* now? Write a text message to a friend.

Example

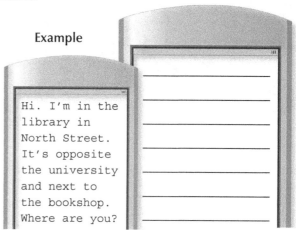

Hi. I'm in the library in North Street. It's opposite the university and next to the bookshop. Where are you?

5 Complete the information about the picture on page 7.

It is a picture of three students ¹ _in_ Amsterdam. Dan is ² _____ the right, and Bob is on the ³ _____. Bob is ⁴ _____ to Dan and ⁵ _____ Ana.

6 〔8〕 Listen and learn the numbers.

13 thirteen	30 thirty	17 seventeen	70 seventy
14 fourteen	40 forty	18 eighteen	80 eighty
15 fifteen	50 fifty	19 nineteen	90 ninety
16 sixteen	60 sixty		100 a hundred
			a hundred and one/two/three

STUDY SKILLS: using your dictionary (1)

1 Match the words with the vowel sounds. Check in your dictionary.

<u>a</u>ren't betw<u>ee</u>n b<u>oa</u>t c<u>a</u>r c<u>e</u>ntre ch<u>ea</u>p dr<u>y</u> <u>eigh</u>t h<u>a</u>rbour h<u>e</u> <u>I</u> l<u>i</u>brary n<u>e</u>xt n<u>o</u> p<u>o</u>st st<u>a</u>tion th<u>ey</u> tw<u>o</u> y<u>e</u>s y<u>ou</u> z<u>oo</u>

1 /eɪ/ _____

2 /iː/ _____

3 /e/ _____

4 /aɪ/ _____

5 /uː/ _____

6 /əʊ/ _____

7 /ɑː/ *aren't* _____

2 Are these sounds the same or different? Check in your dictionary.

1 a) g<u>oo</u>d	b) p<u>oo</u>l	*different*
2 a) g<u>oo</u>d	b) b<u>oo</u>k	*same*
3 a) ch<u>ea</u>p	b) c<u>i</u>ty	_____
4 a) <u>i</u>t	b) th<u>i</u>rty	_____
5 a) L<u>o</u>ndon	b) b<u>u</u>s	_____
6 a) f<u>o</u>rty	b) f<u>ou</u>r	_____
7 a) f<u>o</u>rty	b) b<u>oa</u>t	_____
8 a) <u>o</u>ne	b) b<u>u</u>s	_____

3 Underline the nouns and circle the adjectives in these sentences. Check in your dictionary.

1 This <u>beach</u> is (famous) for <u>surfing</u>.

2 It's cool in September.

3 The water in the pool is warm.

4 There's a good view from the tower.

5 The market is noisy and crowded.

6 There's a bus station and a railway station.

7 There's a good tourist information centre.

WRITING SKILLS: a description of a city

4 Use *and* to join these sentences.

1 There are shops. + There are cafés.

   There are shops and cafés.

2 There's an airport. + There's a railway station.

   _____

3 There are good buses. + There are good trains.

   _____

4 The restaurants are good. + The restaurants are cheap.

   _____

5 It is hot in summer. + It is warm in winter.

   _____

6 The market is noisy. + The restaurants are busy.

   _____

7 There are peaceful parks in the city. + There are beautiful buildings in the city.

   _____

   _____

DICTATION

5 🔲9 Listen and complete the information about a famous capital city in Asia.

A

City: _____

Country: _____

City population: _____

Weather: _____

_____

Tourist information: _____

_____

_____

_____

_____

_____

_____

2 Work and study

2.1 WORKING LIFE

VOCABULARY: jobs and places of work

1 Read the clues and complete the puzzle.

1 They work in offices and use computers.

2 Doctors work in _____.

3 A pilot flies a _____.

4 It sells things.

5 What _____ do you do?

6 A lecturer teaches in a _____.

7 He or she works in a court or an office.

8 They design things.

EXTRA VOCABULARY: families

2 Read about Laura's family and complete the diagram.

Her **mother** is a doctor and her **father** is a lecturer.

Her **brother** is a pilot and her **sister** is a student.

Her **uncle** is a businessman. Her **aunt** does not work.

Her **cousins** are students.

1 Her *mother*

2 Her _____

3 Her _____

4 Her _____

5 Her _____

LAURA

6 Her _____

7 Her _____

GRAMMAR: present simple

3 Write the verb in the correct form.

1 Laura _lives_ (live) in Rome, Italy.

2 Her mother _____ (work) in a hospital.

3 Her brother _____ (fly) a plane.

4 Her aunt _____ (not work).

5 Her cousins _____ (not live) in Rome.

6 Laura _____ (speak) English.

4 Complete the text with the correct form of the verbs in the box.

| doesn't don't don't live like |
| see travel wear ~~work~~ |

Mike doesn't work _in_ an office. He ¹_works_ outside offices. Mike ²_____ in New York and he cleans the windows of big office buildings.

In good weather, Mike ³_____ his job. He says, 'I ⁴_____ a lot of blue sky. It's beautiful up there. I ⁵_____ meet new people in my job, but that's OK. I work with my friend, Sam. We get good money, so we have long vacations and we ⁶_____ to a lot of countries.'

In winter, Mike ⁷_____ like the job because the weather is not good. He ⁸_____ a lot of clothes, but he gets cold and wet. He and Sam ⁹_____ work in very bad weather.

LISTENING

5 🔟 Listen to four people and complete the table.

Person	Where does he/she work?	Does he/she like it?
1	a tourist information office in _____	
2		
3		
4		

LISTEN BETTER

Look at Track 10 on page 78.

Close your book and listen again.

Listening and understanding is good for you!

PRONUNCIATION: -s endings

6 1️⃣1️⃣ Listen to the sound at the end of the words and write _s_, _z_ or _iz_.

Verbs	Plural nouns
1 likes _s_	13 offices _____
2 goes _z_	14 clothes _____
3 uses _iz_	15 shops _____
4 buys _____	16 planes _____
5 wants _____	17 beaches _____
6 manages _____	18 airports _____
7 lives _____	19 doctors _____
8 sells _____	20 lakes _____
9 works _____	21 colleges _____
10 sees _____	22 countries _____
11 speaks _____	23 pilots _____
12 wears _____	24 mountains _____

READING

1a Read the information and the email.

At many British universities, every new student has one or two student 'parents' from Year 2. Student parents write to new students before the course and they help new students in the first week.

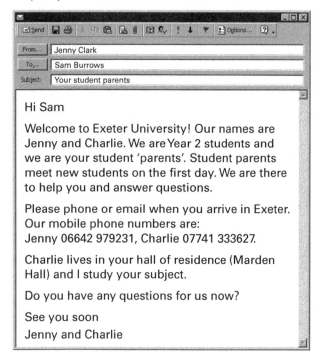

Hi Sam

Welcome to Exeter University! Our names are Jenny and Charlie. We are Year 2 students and we are your student 'parents'. Student parents meet new students on the first day. We are there to help you and answer questions.

Please phone or email when you arrive in Exeter. Our mobile phone numbers are:
Jenny 06642 979231, Charlie 07741 333627.

Charlie lives in your hall of residence (Marden Hall) and I study your subject.

Do you have any questions for us now?

See you soon
Jenny and Charlie

1b Answer the questions.

1 Do student parents write to new students before the course?

   Yes, they do.

2 Do student parents help Year 1 students?

   _____

3 Is Jenny a new student?

   _____

4 Are Jenny and Charlie in Year 2 at the university?

   _____

5 What do student parents do on the first day?

   _____

6 Does Charlie live in Marden Hall?

   _____

7 Does Jenny have a mobile phone?

   _____

2 Complete Sam's reply to his student 'parents'.

From... | Sam Burrows
To... | Jenny Clark
Subject: | RE: Your student parents

Hi Jenny and 1_____

Thank you for your email. Yes, I have two
2_____:

1) Do the halls of residence 3_____ kitchens?
2) 4_____ lectures start on Monday?

Thanks again, and thanks for your mobile phone
5_____. I'll phone when I arrive.

Best wishes
6_____

GRAMMAR:
present simple questions

3 Complete the second sentence so that it means the same as the first.

1 Is there a kitchen in the hall of residence?

   Does the hall of residence *have a kitchen* ?

2 Are there cafés in the halls?

   Do the halls _____?

3 What shops are there on the campus?

   What shops _____ have?

4 Are there computers in the library?

   Does the library _____?

5 Is there a football team in the college?

   _____ have a football team?

6 Is there a railway station in Exeter?

   Does Exeter _____?

7 What language classes are there for foreign students?

   What language classes do _____

   _____?

4 Make questions and answers with these words and *or*.

1 Q: you go   by bus   by car   ?
   A: bus

   Q: *Do you go by bus or by car?*

   A: *I go by bus.*

2 Q: you live   in a hall   a flat   ?
   A: hall
   Q: _____
   _____
   A: _____

3 Q: your brother study   in England   the USA   ?
   A: the USA
   Q: _____
   _____
   A: _____

4 Q: he live   on campus   off campus   ?
   A: on campus
   Q: _____
   _____
   A: _____

5 Q: students have exams   in June   July ?
   A: June
   Q: _____
   _____
   A: _____

TRANSLATION

5 Translate into your language. Notice the differences.

1 What subjects do you study?

_____

2 He doesn't like his job.

_____

3 Do you speak English?

_____

4 My brother has exams in June.

_____

VOCABULARY: student life

6 Which word or phrase does *not* go with the verb? Cross it out.

1 She **studies** ... .

   a) languages b) Chinese c) ~~university~~
   d) in the library

2 A lot of students **do** ... .

   a) sports b) restaurant c) two subjects
   d) a three-year course

3 I **have** ... .

   a) a lot of lessons b) a part-time job
   c) two computers d) colleges

4 Do the students **use** ... ?

   a) dictionaries b) subjects c) the kitchen
   d) English

5 Do you **live** ... ?

   a) in a hall of residence b) in London
   c) with friends d) in exams

6 We **go** ... .

   a) to language classes b) by bus c) to June
   d) to university

7 He **works** ... .

   a) for a big company b) in a restaurant
   c) on a boat d) of a university

SPELLING: words with *-tion*

7 Write the jumbled words correctly. They all contain the letter group *-tion*.

1 ammoccdotiona a c c o m m o d a t i o n
2 seqution q _ _ _ _ _ _ _ _
3 ationqualfici q _ _ _ _ _ _ _ _ _ _ _
4 innatertional i _ _ _ _ _ _ _ _ _ _ _ _
5 tiondicary d _ _ _ _ _ _ _ _ _
6 acudetion e _ _ _ _ _ _ _ _
7 aclippation a _ _ _ _ _ _ _ _ _ _
8 tionast s _ _ _ _ _ _
9 plopuation p _ _ _ _ _ _ _ _
10 contionversa c _ _ _ _ _ _ _ _ _ _ _

VOCABULARY: job advertisements

1a Abbie is a student. She wants a part-time job. Complete the advertisements. Use these words.

| answer | assistant | hour | hours |
| organise | phone | send | ~~skills~~ |

▷ **Job**search

A Do you have good computer [1] _skills_ ?
Lawyer's office needs help with database programme and web design.
One week's work, £8 per [2]_____.
Email ict@sueandgrab.com

B Do you speak Spanish?
Part-time telephone work in the evenings.
[3]_____ 250004

C Saturday job for an [4]_____ in a music shop. Phone 279944.

D We need two office assistants for a busy language school. One to do filing,
[5]_____ emails and
[6]_____ the phone, and
one to [7]_____ events and
accommodation. Working [8]_____:
Monday to Friday 9–5. Phone 272772.

1b Abbie wants to work one day every weekend. Which job is good for her?

KEY LANGUAGE: asking for information (1)

2a Abbie phones about the job. Complete her questions.

1 Can you _tell me_ about the Saturday job, please?

2 Where _____ it?

3 What _____ hours?

4 What _____ salary?

5 What _____ the assistant do?

6 Do I _____ qualifications for this job?

7 What skills _____ need?

2b [12] Listen and check your answers.

3 Listen again and complete Abbie's notes about the job.

> Location: [1] _North Street_
>
> Working hours: [2]_____
>
> Lunch break: [3]_____
>
> Salary: [4]_____
>
> Duties: [5]_____
>
> _____
>
> Qualifications: [6]_____
>
> Skills: [7]_____

DICTATION

4 [13] Listen and write the days of the week.

The weekdays:

1 _ _ _ _ _ _

2 _ _ _ _ _ _ _

3 _ _ _ _ _ _ _ _ _

4 _ _ _ _ _ _ _

5 _ _ _ _ _ _

The weekend:

6 _ _ _ _ _ _ _

7 _ _ _ _ _ _

STUDY SKILLS: using your dictionary (2)

1 Correct the mistakes. Check in your dictionary.

	Stress pattern	Words	Corrections
1	●●	**Nouns:** business ~~degree~~ number office **Other words:** answer design modern visit	_____ _____
2	●●	**Nouns:** country CV event guitar **Other words:** about begin between practise	*degree* _____
3	●●●	**Nouns:** Arabic computer hospital salary **Other words:** beautiful expensive organise	_____ _____
4	●●●	**Nouns:** assistant employment professor telephone **Other words:** official remember wonderful	_____ _____

2 Complete the table with the 'other words' from Exercise 1. Check in your dictionary.

Verb and noun	Verb	Adjective	Preposition
answer			

WRITING SKILLS: an application form

3 Which words need capital letters? Underline the words.

<u>peter</u> <u>jones</u> is 23 and <u>british</u>. <u>he</u> is a web designer and he works for a small company in <u>manchester</u>. its name is webcom designs. he lives in banbury road, manchester, at house number 47. he has a ba degree in typography and design from london university and he speaks two foreign languages: french (advanced) and spanish (intermediate). peter doesn't like manchester. he likes london and has a lot of friends there. he wants a new job in london. he wants to work for superweb. superweb is a big company with offices in london and new york.

4 Complete this form for Peter Jones.

Superweb Job Application Form

Name: 1_____

Address: 2_____

_____

Nationality: 3_____

Date of birth: 4 *25/01/*_____

Present employment: 5_____

_____

Education/Training: 6_____

_____

Languages: 7_____

_____

3 Water

3.1 WET AND DRY

1 Choose the best word, a), b) or c), to complete the sentences.

1 Water _boils_ at 100°C.
   a) boils   b) cooks   c) washes

2 What do you _____ in the morning?
   a) swim   b) sleep   c) drink

3 How do you _____ coffee?
   a) change   b) make   c) stop

4 At what temperature does water _____?
   a) find   b) waste   c) freeze

READING

2 Skim this web page for one minute. Then answer the questions.

1 What is the main topic of the page?
   _____

2 Are there two questions or three questions?
   _____

3 Which questions are interesting for _you_?
   _____

HOME   ARTICLES   NEWS   A-Z INDEX   FAQs   CONTACTS   LINKS   SEARCH 🔍 _____

▶ **Deserts** _Dr Steve Simmonds answers your questions._

---

1 How do plants get water in hot dry deserts?

Good question. There is almost no rain in deserts, but there is water. You don't see this water in the daytime, but you see it in the early morning. In deserts, the nights are cold. At the end of the night, there is dew on the plants and on the ground. So the plants get a little water at night.

⟩ DEW ON A PLANT

2 Why don't camels need water in the desert?

Camels need a lot of water. Camels sometimes drink 90 litres of water in 10 minutes! But after that, they can drink nothing for a week. Most animals need water every day, but camels do not.

3 What percentage of the world is desert?

Deserts cover about 20% of the world's land. Deserts, as you know, are very dry areas, but they are not all hot. Some deserts are very cold. The Sahara is an example of a hot desert and Antarctica is an example of a cold desert.

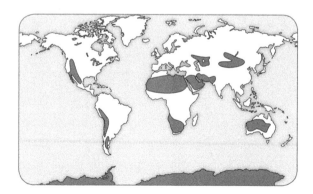

3 Read the web page again. Are these sentences true or false?

1 Deserts have no rain. *false*

2 In deserts, the temperature goes up at night.

3 Desert plants get water from dew.

4 Camels can drink nine litres of water in one minute.

5 Camels need water every day.

6 Deserts are wet areas.

7 Some deserts are cold and some are hot.

WRITING

4 Rewrite the 'false' sentences from Exercise 3. Make them true.

1 *(1) Deserts have almost no rain.*

2 _____

   _____

3 _____

   _____

4 _____

   _____

GRAMMAR: question words

5 Complete the questions with the question words in the box.

| How What When Where |
| Which ~~Who~~ Why |

1 Q: 1 *Who* is he?
  A: He's my cousin.

2 Q: _____ does he live?
  A: He lives in London.

3 Q: _____ does he do?
  A: He's a pilot.

4 Q: _____ is the English lesson?
  A: It's on Monday.

5 Q: _____ do you travel to work?
  A: By car.

6 Q: _____ do you want: tea or coffee?
  A: Tea, please.

7 Q: _____ don't you swim?
  A: The water's cold!

6 Complete the questions about deserts.

1 Q: *When do* desert animals look for food?
  A: They look for food at night.

2 Q: _____ a lot of animals do in the day?
  A: They sleep.

3 Q: _____ the Sahara desert?
  A: It's in Africa.

4 Q: _____ do people _____ in the Sahara?
  A: People travel by car or they ride on camels.

5 Q: _____ the Tuareg?
  A: They are people of the Sahara Desert.

6 Q: _____ the temperature fall in the Sahara?
  A: It falls at night.

7 Q: _____ desert _____ in South America: the Patagonian Desert or the Sahara Desert?
  A: The Patagonian Desert.

8 Q: _____ doesn't Europe have a desert?
  A: Because Europe has a lot of rain.

SPELLING AND PRONUNCIATION: silent letters

7a [14] Listen to these words.

w̲ho w̲here k̲now desig̲n.

The underlined letters are silent (= We do not pronounce them).

7b [15] Listen to these sentences. Write the words with silent letters. Circle the silent letters.

1 What do you know about it? _W(h)at_ _(k)now_

2 Listen and answer. _____ _____

3 Do you write with your right hand?

   _____ _____

4 Who is your friend? _____ _____

5 He is a foreign businessman.

   _____ _____

6 We study Chemistry at school.

   _____ _____

7 She talks for hours! _____ _____

VOCABULARY:
words connected with water

1 Match these words with gaps 1–6.

dive   jump   float   lake   ocean   sea

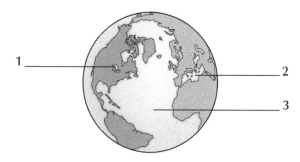

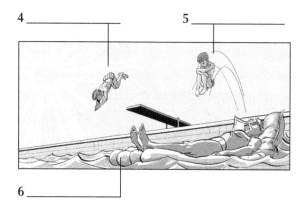

VOCABULARY:
words from the lesson

2 Match nouns 1–6 with a–e.

1 length	a) 40 kilograms
2 weight	b) 25%
3 temperature	c) 90
4 number	d) 6 metres
5 percentage	e) often
6 frequency	f) 35°C

3 Choose the correct word to complete the sentences.

1 Baby whales drink 230 litres *for/of/to* milk a day.

2 Dolphins often jump *up/out/off* of the water.

3 These whales live *at/to/in* the Atlantic Ocean.

4 We always see whales *on/in/by* the trips.

5 They are sometimes *near/between/next* the boat.

6 What percentage *of/in/to* an iceberg is under water?

7 Water boils *in/at/for* a temperature of 100°C.

8 Humpback whales are famous *for/of/to* their jumps.

GRAMMAR:
adverbs of frequency

4 Choose the best word or phrase, a), b) or c), to complete the sentences.

1 We see dolphins _every day_ .

   a) never   b) not often   c) every day

2 Dolphins _____ dangerous.

   a) are never   b) never   c) never are

3 Dolphins _____ swim with other dolphins.

   a) weekly   b) usually   c) every day

4 They _____ out of the water.

   a) sometimes jump   b) jump always   c) often

5 They eat fish, but _____ eat other dolphins.

   a) never they   b) they are never   c) they never

6 Small dolphins sometimes play with other small dolphins. We see that about _____.

   a) once a month   b) occasionally   c) never

7 We do trips _____ times a week.

   a) once   b) twice   c) three

5 Write and answer questions with *How often*.

1 Q: _How often do_ penguins visit the Antarctic?

   A: (every winter)

   They visit the Antarctic every winter.

2 Q: _____ you go to the beach?

   A: (twice a year)

   _____

3 Q: _____ they go in a boat?

   A: (almost never)

   _____

4 Q: _____ she buy an English newspaper?

   A: (once or twice a week)

   _____

   _____

5 Q: _____ he swim in the sea?

   A: (often)

   _____

TRANSLATION

6 Translate into your language. Notice the differences.

1 What do you usually do at the weekend?

_____

2 She has English lessons twice a week.

_____

3 Why do dolphins jump out of the water?

_____

LISTENING

7 🔲16 Listen to the lecture and complete the information.

There are about ¹_____ different kinds of shark.

Three examples:

A The Great White Shark

Maximum length: ²_____

Food: ³_____

Dangerous? ⁴_____

B The Whale Shark

Maximum length: ⁵_____

Food: ⁶_____

Dangerous? ⁷_____

C The Pygmy Shark

Maximum length: ⁸_____

Food: ⁹_____

Dangerous? ¹⁰_____

WRITING

8 Complete the summary about sharks.

¹_____ about 400 kinds of shark. One example is the Great ²_____. It has a maximum ³_____. It eats fish and ⁴_____ and it is ⁵_____ to people.

Another example is the Whale Shark. It ⁶_____ 12 metres. It ⁷_____ sea animals. It never attacks people, so it ⁸_____ to people.

DICTATION

9 🔲17 Listen and complete the information about sharks.

People say sharks are dangerous, but about _____ _____ kill people.

_____

_____

_____

_____

_____

VOCABULARY: festivals

1 Complete the text about a festival in Venice, Italy, with the words in the box.

> children   music   races   ~~takes place~~
> teams   traditional   watch   wear

This festival [1] *takes place* every year in September. It starts with a parade of [2]_____ boats on the Grand Canal. The people in the boats [3]_____ traditional clothes. After that, there are boat races. The first races are for [4]_____. Then there are [5]_____ for women and races for men in [6]_____ of six. A lot of people [7]_____ the races, and they make a lot of noise. In the evening, there are shows and [8]_____ all night.

KEY LANGUAGE: making suggestions

2a Complete the missing words in this conversation about a different festival.

ALICE: The festival is on Sunday. There are races and shows, good food and good music.

BEN: That sounds fun. I'd [1]*like* to go to it.

CLAIRE: Me, too.

DAN: Yes. [2]L_____ go and see it.

BEN: Good [3]i_____.

CLAIRE: When does it start?

ALICE: About midday.

BEN: OK. Why [4]d_____ we meet there?

CLAIRE: Great! [5]H_____ about meeting there at 12?

DAN: That sounds good.

BEN: I'm not so [6]s_____. It starts at 12, so [7]w_____ about meeting at 11.30?

CLAIRE: 11.30? That means getting a bus at 10.30.

DAN: And that means getting up at nine o'clock. I don't [8]w_____ to do that.

ALICE: [9]W_____ don't you all come in my car? It's only 20 minutes by car.

CLAIRE: That sounds good.

DAN: Excellent! Thanks.

BEN: OK. So, it's 11.10 at your house.

ALICE: [10]L_____ say 11.15.

BEN: OK. See you then.

2b ▪18▪ Listen and check your answers.

STUDY SKILLS: classroom language

1 Choose the correct sentence, a) or b).

1 a) What does *evaporate* mean?
   b) ~~What means *evaporate*?~~

2 a) How you spell *vapour*?
   b) How do you spell *vapour*?

3 a) What do you pronounce *cycle*?
   b) How do you pronounce *cycle*?

4 a) Can you repeat again, please?
   b) Can you say that again, please?

5 a) What do you mean?
   b) What you mean?

6 a) I don't understand.
   b) I no understand.

EXTRA LANGUAGE:
this, that, these, those

2 Look at the pictures and complete the answers.

1 What's this in English?   3 What are these in English?

It's a *whale* .   They're _____ .

2 What's that in English?   4 What are those in English?

It's a _____ .   They're _____ .

**3 Complete the questions about these things. Use
this, that, these or *those*.**

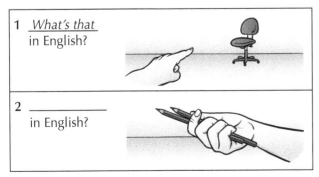

1 *What's that*
   in English?

2 _____
   in English?

3 _____
   in English?

4 _____
   in English?

WRITING SKILLS:
a description of a process

4 Complete the text with the words in the box.

| and | becomes | changes | finally |
| heats | it | that | then | they |

How to get water in a hot dry desert.

You need a clear plastic bag. Put the bag over a
green plant and close [1]_____ . After
about four hours, there is water in the bag. Why?

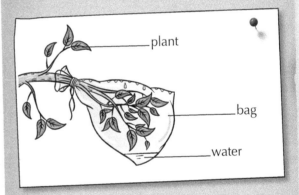

plant

bag

water

Plants always have water in them.
[2]_____ get this water from
dew [3]_____ from the ground.
In the daytime, the sun [4]_____
the plant. Water in the plant evaporates and
[5]_____ water vapour.
[6]_____ the vapour in the bag
[7]_____ into water. After
[8]_____ , the water in the bag
falls to the bottom of the bag. It forms a pool
of water at the bottom of the bag. This process
continues for a few hours. [9]_____ ,
the pool of water is big enough to drink.

4 Leisure time

4.1 SILVER SCREEN

LISTEN BETTER

English speakers **stress** one or two words in every sentence.
Example: *It's a **comedy** film. It's about a **police** officer.*
Listen for the stressed words.

1 `19` A customer is choosing a film. Listen to the conversation and complete the tables.

Film 1

a) Type of film	_____
b) It's about	a _____. He runs from the police because they think he's a killer.
c) She thinks it's	good and very _____.

Film 2

a) Type of film	_____
b) It's about	an _____. He has a _____ in Casablanca.
c) She thinks it's	a _____ film.

GRAMMAR: articles

2 Choose the correct words to complete the film reviews.

▪▪▪▪▪▪▪▪▪▪▪▪▪▪▪▪ Film **Reviews** ▪▪

Films | Features | Interviews | Now showing | Games

TITANIC
★ ★ ★ ★ ★
It's ¹*a/an* Hollywood blockbuster about a big ship and ²*a/an* iceberg. You know ³*a/the* name of the ship. A rich girl and ⁴*a/the* poor boy meet on the ship, and ⁵*a/the* film is really about them. It's ⁶*a/an* exciting and beautiful film.

KING KONG
★ ★ ★ ★ ★
⁷*Films / The films* about animals are not usually blockbusters, but this one is different. One of the top films of 2005, this is the story of ⁸*big / a big*, dangerous animal – a <u>very</u> big, <u>very</u> dangerous animal – in ⁹*New York / the New York*. ¹⁰*A/The* film is three hours long but very exciting.

---

3 Complete the sentences with *a*, *an*, *the* or no article (write Ø).

Film A

This is ¹ *an* old film but a big favourite.
²_____ man rides into town. Who is he? He has no name. There are ³_____ bad men in the town. He meets the bad men. He is fast, and ⁴_____ bad men die. The man with no name rides out of town.

Film B

This new children's film is about ⁵_____ eleven-year-old boy and ⁶_____ visitor from a different world. The visitor meets the boy and lives in the boy's home, but ⁷_____ boy's parents don't know. What happens when the boy's mother finds the visitor? Watch ⁸_____ film and see!

VOCABULARY: types of film

4 Match the films in the reviews in Exercises 2 and 3 with the types of film, a–d.

1 Titanic
2 King Kong
3 Film A
4 Film B

a) an action/adventure film
b) a western
c) a science fiction film
d) a love story

5 Match the clues, 1–3, with the types of film, a–c.

1 It's about the past.
2 There aren't any actors in it.
3 Don't watch it late at night!

a) an animation
b) a horror film
c) a historical film

VOCABULARY: words connected with films

6a Read the clues and complete the puzzle.

1 These people work in the film industry. Some of them are very rich and famous.
2 You watch films in this building.
3 This person tells actors what to do.
4 Romantic comedy is a type of _____.
5 Actors and directors _____ films.
6 Famous actors
7 This type of film is often about 'Who is the killer?'. The word rhymes with *killer*.
8 What is the film _____?
9 The opposite of *famous* or *unusual*.
10 This type of film has a lot of songs.

1			a				
2		c					
3			d				
4		c					
5			m				
6			s				
7	t						
8		a					
9	o						
10		m					

↑

6b What is the mystery word?

PRONUNCIATION: /ð/

7 [20] Listen and study the diagram. Practise saying the sound /ð/ in *the, this* and *that*.

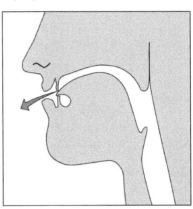

8a [21] Listen to these words. Which sound do you hear? Write a or b.

a) /ðə/
b) /ði/

1 the film _a_
2 the actors _b_
3 the director ____
4 the animation ____
5 the cinema ____
6 the other film ____
7 the iceberg ____
8 the ship ____

> Before a vowel, *the* has a long sound /ði/.
> Before a consonant, it is /ðə/.

8b Listen again and repeat.

SPELLING: -er or -or?

9 Complete the words with *-er* or *-or*.

1 thrill*er*
2 horr*or*
3 act____
4 direct____
5 manag____
6 teach____
7 profess____
8 lectur____
9 lawy____
10 doct____

1 Choose the best word, a), b) or c), to complete the sentences.

1 Can you _play_ football?
   a) play   b) go   c) do

2 How often do you _____ running?
   a) play   b) go   c) make

3 She _____ aerobics once a week.
   a) goes   b) does   c) plays

4 Do you want to play tennis or _____ something different?
   a) make   b) go   c) do

5 Can you _____?
   a) swim   b) yoga   c) basketball

6 How often do you _____ to a fitness club?
   a) go   b) use   c) do

7 Can you _____ a bike?
   a) drive   b) ride   c) go

GRAMMAR: can, can't

2 Complete the questions with *can* and the words in brackets. Complete the answers.

1 Q: (you run) _Can you run_ for 15 minutes?
   A: No, _I can't_. I _____ run for two minutes but not 15!

2 Q: (you ski) _____?
   A: Yes, _____.

3 Q: (she ride) _____ a horse?
   A: No, _____, but she _____ ride a bike.

4 Q: (he lift) What weight _____?
   A: He _____ 80 kilograms.

5 Q: (you play) Which sports _____?
   A: We _____ tennis and football, and I _____ play basketball, but he _____ basketball.

3 You are a new member of a fitness club. Complete the questions. Use *can*.

1 You want to find a timetable of classes.
   Where _can I find a timetable of classes_?

2 You want to buy a coffee.
   Where _____?

3 You want to use the swimming pool.
   When _____?

4 You want to watch sports on TV.
   Where _____?

5 You want to do an aerobics class.
   When _____?

6 You and a friend want to learn yoga.
   How _____?

7 You and a friend want to become full members
   How _____?

EXTRA VOCABULARY: dimensions

4 Complete the sentences with *deep, high, long* or *wide*.

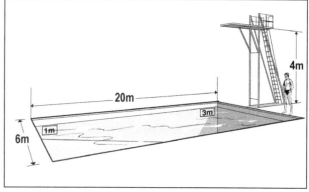

1 The pool is 3 metres _deep_ at the deep end.
2 The diving board is 4 metres _____.
3 The mountain is 2,000 metres _____.
4 The park is two kilometres _____ and half a kilometre _____.
5 The sea here is 20 metres _____.

READING AND LISTENING

5a [22] **Read and listen to the opinions.**

Opinion A

I like keeping fit, but I don't go to a fitness club. Why pay a lot of money to use running machines, cycling machines and rowing machines and do yoga classes? I can do yoga at home, I can run in a beautiful park near my home and I can cycle around the city. With that money I can go rowing on a river. So why go rowing on a machine? That's boring!

Opinion B

I like running, cycling and tennis, but I can't do these activities outside in bad weather. I like swimming too, but I don't live near the sea. So I go to a fitness club three times a week. It's great! There are a lot of machines and equipment, I can use the swimming pool and I can learn new things in the classes. I can relax and meet friends in the club's café, too.

5b **Answer the questions, *Yes* or *No*.**

1 Does the woman go to a fitness club? *no*

2 Does she think fitness clubs are expensive?

3 Does she live near a park?

4 Can the man always go running outside?

5 Can he swim in the sea near his home?

6 Does he go to the fitness club every day?

7 Does he like meeting friends at the club?

WRITING

6 **What do you think about opinions A and B? Underline your answer.**

I agree with A.

I agree with B.

I'm not sure.

7 **Write about *you*. Answer these questions.**

What activities do you like?
Do you go to a fitness club?
What can you do?

_____

_____

_____

_____

_____

_____

_____

_____

TRANSLATION

8 **Translate into your language. Notice the differences with *can* and articles (*a/the*).**

1 The club has a pool.

_____

2 Can part-time members use the pool?

_____

3 Clubs are expensive. I can't pay £50 a month.

_____

_____

VOCABULARY: holiday travel

1 Which word or phrase is *not* correct? Cross it out.

1 Can we swim in the *sea/pool/~~beach~~*?

2 Let's stay in a *hotel/museum/chalet*.

3 I like to try *different food / new sports / new friends*.

4 Do you have a *sea/double/family* room?

5 Let's go *to a restaurant / for a walk / with a sea view*.

6 This is a picture of me on *the beach / a motorbike / the hotel*.

KEY LANGUAGE: asking for information (2), saying *no* politely

2a Complete the conversation at a hotel between a hotel worker and a visitor.

H: Hello. ¹ *Can* I help you?

V: Yes, please. Can you ²_____ me some information ³_____ the hotel's facilities?

H: Yes, of ⁴_____. What would you ⁵_____ to ⁶_____?

V: ⁷_____ there a fitness club in the hotel?

H: Yes, ⁸_____ is. It's on the first floor.

V: Is it open now?

H: No, I'm ⁹_____ not. It closes at 7 p.m.

V: ¹⁰_____ we play tennis now?

H: I'm ¹¹_____. I'm afraid you ¹²_____. Tennis closes at 7, too.

2b ▨ 23 ▨ Listen and check your answers.

3 Complete the answers with *I'm afraid* + verb.

1 Q: Do the rooms have satellite TV?

   A: No, *I'm afraid they don't* .

2 Q: Does the hotel have a swimming pool?

   A: No, _____.

3 Q: Is the hotel near the beach?

   A: No, _____.

4 Q: Can we use the gym?

   A: No, _____.

5 Q: Is there another hotel near here?

   A: No, _____.

6 Q: Are there any campsites?

   A: I'm sorry. _____.

EXTRA LANGUAGE: possessive *s*

4 Study these sentences and the information.

Are there any children's activities?
Is there a kids' club?

> *children's activities* = activities for children
> *a kids' club* = a club for kids
> *a lawyer's office* = an office of a lawyer
> *lawyers' offices* = offices of lawyers

Choose the correct word to complete the sentences.

1 What is the *hotel's/~~hotels'~~* telephone number?

2 Edinburgh is *Scotland's/Scotlands'* capital city.

3 Travel agents answer *customer's/customers'* questions.

4 They are *Kate's/Kates'* brothers.

5 Lisa is at a hotel with her mother and father. *Lisa's/Lisas'* room has a sea view, but her *parent's/parents'* room does not.

6 Our *friend's/friends'* rooms are 302, 303 and 324.

7 My *cousin's/cousins'* room is very nice but he doesn't like it.

1 Write the numbers in order of size (big to small).

nine million, six hundred and sixty thousand
four hundred and fifty thousand
ninety-nine thousand, nine hundred and ninety-nine
ninety million
eight hundred thousand
seven hundred and forty-four

1 _90,000,000_   4 _____

2 _____   5 _____

3 _____   6 _744_

2 Write the fractions and percentages.

1 a quarter _¼_

2 thirty percent _30%_

3 a half _____

4 fifty-six percent _____

5 two-thirds _____

6 seventeen percent _____

7 three-fifths _____

8 seventy percent _____

3 Look at the pie chart. Choose the correct words to complete the text.

Favourite films

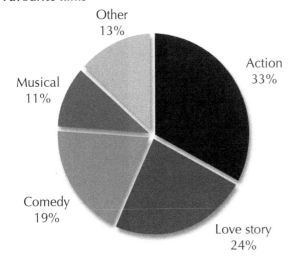

Other 13%
Action 33%
Musical 11%
Comedy 19%
Love story 24%

¹About/Over/Exactly a third of these films are action films and ²about/over/exactly a quarter are love stories. ³Nearly/Over/Exactly 20% are comedies. ⁴Exactly/Nearly/Over 10% are musicals and ⁵over/about/exactly 13% are other types.

4 We use ordinal numbers for fractions:

⅓ (a third), ⅖ (two-fifths)

and dates:

3rd June (the third of June).

1st / first	8th / eighth	15th / fifteenth
2nd / second	9th / ninth	16th / sixteenth
3rd / third	10th / tenth	17th / seventeenth
4th / fourth	11th / eleventh	18th / eighteenth
5th / fifth	12th / twelfth	19th / nineteenth
6th / sixth	13th / thirteenth	20th / twentieth
7th / seventh	14th / fourteenth	21st / twenty-first

Write these fractions and dates in words.

1 ⅔ _two-thirds_

2 6th May _____

3 ⁹⁄₁₀ _____

4 2nd April _____

5 ⅛ _____

6 18th August _____

7 ¹⁄₁₂ _____

8 21st July _____

9 22nd June _____

10 31st January _____

5 24 Listen and complete the information about British people's travel. Use correct punctuation.

People in Britain make _____

visits to other countries per year. _____

_____

_____

_____

_____

_____

_____

_____

5 Transport

5.1 SPEED

VOCABULARY: transport

1 Put the means of transport in order of …

1 speed. | lorry ship plane car |

  1 *plane*   3 _____

  2 *car*   4 _____

2 size. | lorry train motorbike taxi |

  1 _____ 3 _____

  2 _____ 4 _____

3 price per kilometre. | train taxi bike plane |

  1 _____ 3 _____

  2 _____ 4 _____

4 comfort. | car motorbike bike tram |

  1 _____ 3 _____

  2 _____ 4 _____

GRAMMAR: comparative adjectives

2 Choose the correct word or phrase in sentences 1–4.

1 Planes are faster *than/that* cars.

2 Trains are *big/bigger* than lorries.

3 A bike is *cheaper / more cheap* than a taxi.

4 A tram is *comfortable / more comfortable* than a bike.

3 Compare cars and motorbikes. Write six sentences. Use the words in the boxes.

Cars	Motorbikes
comfortable	exciting
good in wet weather	fast in cities
expensive to buy	dangerous

1 *Cars are more comfortable than motorbikes.*

2 _____

3 _____

4 _____

5 _____

6 _____

4 Answer the questions. Use *than*.

1 Q: Which is bigger: a jumbo or a superjumbo?

  A: *A superjumbo is bigger than a jumbo.*

2 Q: Which is faster: a tram or a train?

  A: _____

3 Q: Which is easier to drive: a car or a lorry?

  A: _____

4 Q: Which are more popular: cars or motorbikes?

  A: _____

5 Q: Which are longer: trams or trains?

  A: _____

5 Answer the questions. Use the correct form of the words in the box + *than*.

big cheap comfortable expensive fast old

1 Q: What is the difference between a ship and a boat?

  A: *A ship is bigger than a boat.*

2 Q: What is the difference between an ordinary train and a high-speed train?

  A: _____

  _____

3 Q: What are the differences between the mountain bike (A) and the town bike (B)?

  (A)   (B)

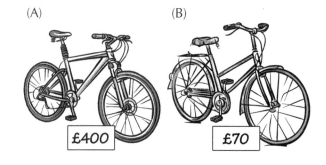

£400   £70

  A: The town bike is _____ and _____

  _____.

  The mountain bike is _____

  and _____

  _____.

EXTRA VOCABULARY: colours

6 Write the colours in the correct gaps.

| black blue brown green grey |
| ~~red~~ silver white yellow |

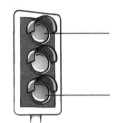

1 *red*

2 _____

3 _____

4 _____

5 _____

6 _____

7 _____

8 _____

9 _____

7 Find coloured things in your Course book.

page _40_ _a yellow car_   page ___ _____

page ___ _____   page ___ _____

page ___ _____   page ___ _____

page ___ _____   page ___ _____

LISTENING

8 `25` Listen and complete the tables.

Popular car colours this year		
	In the USA	In the UK
1	*silver*	
2		
3		
4		
5		
6		

Dangerous colours?	Safer colours?

9 Answer the questions.

1 Which colours are popular colours for cars in *your* country?

_____

2 Which colour(s) do *you* like for cars?

_____

PRONUNCIATION: vowel sounds

10a Which vowel sound is different? Cross it out.

1 WHITE /aɪ/   a) bike b) by c) ~~train~~

2 GREY /eɪ/   a) plane b) train c) buy

3 GREEN /iː/   a) ship b) cheap c) sea

4 BLUE /uː/   a) you b) slow c) do

5 BROWN /aʊ/   a) how b) phone c) noun

10b `26` Listen and check your answers.

GRAMMAR: superlative adjectives

1 Match the titles a–d with the texts 1–4.

> a) The world's busiest train company
> b) The world's largest station
> c) The biggest passenger ship in the world
> d) The most expensive bike

1 _b_ It is about 100 years old and it is in New York. Over 200,000 passengers and 550 trains use it every day. It can hold 67 trains at one time.

2 ___ It is 139 metres long and 59 metres wide. It can carry 5,740 people. It takes tourists from Miami, Florida, to the Caribbean Sea.

3 ___ It weighs only 9 kilograms but it costs $12,000. It is strong and fast. Its rider uses it for off-road races.

4 ___ It carries 16 million passengers per day. Many of the passengers live in the Tokyo area or travel to and from Tokyo every day.

2 Choose the best expression, a), b) or c), to complete the sentences.

1 _The biggest_ station in the world is in New York.

a) The big   b) The bigger   c) The biggest

2 Boston has _____ underground train system in North America.

a) the oldest   b) older than   c) oldest

3 Racing bikes are _____ than mountain bikes.

a) the fastest   b) faster   c) fastest

4 Buses are cheaper than taxis, but taxis are _____ comfortable.

a) most   b) more   c) the

5 Air travel is one of _____ safest types of travel.

a) the most   b) the more   c) the

6 _____ dangerous part of air travel is the drive to the airport.

a) More   b) Most   c) The most

7 The _____ colour for cars in the USA is silver.

a) more popular b) most   c) most popular

3a Read the information about a very common word.

> One of the most common nouns in English is the word 'way'. We often use it with superlative adjectives.
>
> **way = route or direction**
> *Can you tell me the quickest way to the station?*
> *Where is the nearest way in / way out?*
> **way = method**
> *The best way to get around Paris is the metro.*
> *The quickest way to learn English is to go to England.*

3b Complete the sentences. Use the superlative form of the word in brackets + *way*.

1 Q: What's the _best way_ (good) to get to the airport?

A: The _____ (quick) is by taxi,

but the _____ (cheap) is by bus.

2 Q: What's the best way to get to New York?

A: The _____ (fast) is by plane.

The _____ (relaxing) is by ship.

3 Q: Can you tell me the way to the city centre?

A: Do you want the _____ (easy)

or the _____ (interesting)?

TRANSLATION

4 Translate into your language. Notice the differences.

1 It is the biggest train station in the world.

_____

2 It is the most expensive way to travel.

_____

3 This car is cheaper than the other two cars.

_____

4 This car is the cheapest of the three.

_____

READING

READ BETTER

This text has three paragraphs.

Always think *'What is the paragraph mainly about?'*

5 Read the text about San Francisco's cable cars and choose a) or b).

1 Paragraph 1 is mainly about _b_ .
   a) The people of San Francisco
   b) San Francisco's transport system

2 Paragraph 2 is mainly about ___.
   a) cable cars
   b) trams and how they work

3 Paragraph 3 is mainly about ___.
   a) where?
   b) why?

6 Are these sentences about the text true or false?

1 Only one city uses cable cars for city transport. *true*

2 Cables pull trams and cable cars.

3 Cable cars have electric motors.

4 The cable car system is not new.

5 The cable cars are popular and good for tourism.

SPELLING: e, ee and ea

7 'e' is the most common letter in English. Which words need e at the end? Write e or Ø (for no e).

1 ship__Ø__   7 bus__

2 bik__e__   8 peopl__

3 taxi__   9 rid__

4 driv__   10 travel__

5 saf__   11 hav__

6 nic__   12 expensiv__

8 Make words with ee or ea.

1 ch__e__ __a__ p

2 sp __ __ d

3 str __ __ t

4 y __ __ r

5 s __ __

6 s __ __

7 n __ __ ds

8 b __ __ utiful

San Francisco's cable cars

People in San Francisco, USA, have an unusual way of getting around the city centre. San Francisco is the only city in the world with a cable car system. There are 39 cable cars. They cover 16 kilometres of roads and they carry over 12 million passengers a year.

Cable cars are different from trams. Trams have electric motors but cable cars do not have motors. They work in a different way. Cables under the streets pull the 'cars' and one big electric motor pulls all the cables. At only 14kph, cable cars are slower than trams.

These cables pull the 'cars'.

The system is very old and San Francisco is a modern city, but the people of San Francisco like the old system. It is also good for business. Tourists like the traditional cable cars and the city's Cable Car Museum is one of its most popular tourist attractions.

SCENARIO: At a ticket agency

VOCABULARY: air travel

1 Put these words in the correct gaps.

> aisle arrival business departure drinks
> flight attendants hand luggage passengers
> snacks standard tickets window

1 Two types of seat:

an _aisle_ seat and a _____ seat

2 People on a plane:

_____ and _____

3 In-flight services:

_____ and _____

4 Passengers have these things with them:

_____ and _____

5 Two classes of ticket:

_____ class and _____
class

6 The beginning and the end of a flight:

_____ and _____

KEY LANGUAGE: buying a ticket

2a What can you say to a ticket agent in these situations? Complete the sentences with two words.

1 You want to know about flights to Tokyo.

Can you tell _me_ _about_ flights to Tokyo?

2 You want to know the cost of the flight.

How _____ _____ the flight cost?

3 You want to know the departure time of the evening flight.

When _____ the evening flight _____?

4 You want to know about cheaper flights.

Are _____ _____ cheaper flights?

5 You want to know the length of the cheaper flight.

How _____ _____ the cheaper flight take?

6 You want to book the cheaper flight.

I'd _____ _____ book the cheaper flight.

2b 🔲27 Listen and check your answers.

3a You are a ticket agent. How do you ask about these things? Complete the questions.

1 The customer's date of travel

When do _____?

2 The type of ticket (business class or standard class?)

Would you _____?

3 The customer's name

Can I _____?

4 How the customer wants to pay

How _____?

3b 🔲28 Listen and check your answers.

EXTRA VOCABULARY: the time

4a Study the chart.

24-hour		12-hour	
0800	oh eight hundred	8 a.m.	eight o'clock
1330	thirteen thirty	1.30 p.m.	one thirty *or* half past one
1345	thirteen forty-five	1.45 p.m.	one forty-five *or* quarter to two

4b Complete the sentences. Use the 12-hour system.

1 Q: What time does the bus leave?

A: It leaves at six _o'clock_ .

2 Q: What time is it now?

A: It's quarter _____.

3 Q: What _____ is the flight?

A: Nine _____.

4 Q: _____ time does it arrive?

A: Quarter _____.

5 Q: _____ is the meeting?

A: Half _____.

6 Q: What time _____ now?

A: It's five _____.

1 Topic sentences
Complete the topic sentences for three paragraphs. Use information from the chart.

The world's biggest and busiest airports	
Airport	**has the largest ...**
Hartsfield, USA	number of passengers.
London Heathrow, UK	number of international passengers.
King Khalid, Saudi Arabia	size.

Topic sentence for paragraph 1

The busiest airport in the world is _Hartsfield_ airport in the _____.

Topic sentence for paragraph 2

The airport with the largest number of international passengers is _____ in the _____.

Topic sentence for paragraph 3

These two airports, Hartsfield and Heathrow, are not the biggest in the world: _____ airport in _____ is bigger than both of them.

2 These are the sentences in paragraph 1. Number them in the best order.

a) Chicago O'Hare Airport, also in the USA, is the second busiest, with 75 million passengers per year. ☐

b) Over 80 million passengers per year pass through it, many of them from other cities in the USA. ☐

c) The busiest airport in the world is Hartsfield airport in the USA. ☐ 1

d) The third busiest is London Heathrow with nearly 70 million passengers per year. ☐

e) Hartsfield is the main airport for the city of Atlanta. ☐

3 Choose the correct words to complete paragraphs 2 and 3.

The airport with the largest number of international passengers is London Heathrow in the UK. From [1]*this/~~these~~* airport planes fly to over 90 countries [2]*and/but* you can fly to over 180 destinations in those countries. London [3]*also/and* has four smaller international airports. [4]*So/But* London, with five international airports, is the world's busiest centre for air travel.

[5]*This/These* two airports, Hartsfield and Heathrow, are not the biggest in the world: King Khalid airport in Saudi Arabia is bigger than both of them. [6]*An/The* airport is in Riyadh, the capital of Saudi Arabia. [7]*It/They* is more than 200 square kilometres in size [8]*and/but* is larger than many cities. The airport has four terminals [9]*and/but* people use only three of them. London Heathrow is busier than this airport [10]*and/but* is only one-twentieth of its size.

4 29 Listen and write about speed limits. Use correct punctuation.

Maximum speed limits on fast roads are _____
_____
_____
_____
_____
_____
_____
_____

6 Food

6.1 SUPER FOOD

VOCABULARY: food and drink

1 Choose the best food, a), b) or c), to complete the sentences.

1 _Oranges_ grow on trees.
   a) Noodles b) ~~Oranges~~ c) Carrots

2 British people often put _____ in tea.
   a) milk b) bananas c) garlic

3 _____ is a green vegetable.
   a) Nuts b) Strawberries c) Broccoli

4 We get _____ from the seas and oceans.
   a) sardines b) red peppers c) bread

5 We get _____ from rivers and fish farms.
   a) rice b) olive oil c) salmon

2 Complete the sentence with *fruit* and *vegetable*.

seeds

For a cook, a tomato is a ¹_____ but for a scientist it is a type of ²_____ because it has seeds in it.

SPELLING: double and single consonants

3 Write four words from Exercise 1 in each box.

Double consonants	No double consonants
carrots	bananas

GRAMMAR: countable and uncountable nouns, *some* and *any*

4 Choose the correct words to complete the sentences.

1 Oranges *has/have* vitamin C.

2 India sells *banana/bananas* to other countries.

3 *Vegetable/Vegetables* are good for you.

4 Do you want *a/some* rice?

5 Milk *is/are* good for you.

6 *Is/Are* olive oil more expensive than milk?

7 We don't have *some/any* strawberries.

5 What is in the picture? Choose the correct words.

There are some ¹*strawberry/strawberries*, ²*an/some* ice cream, some ³*orange/oranges* and ⁴*some/a* banana.

6 Make sentences about Sam. Match 1–6 with a–f.

1 Sam spends money fast. So today he does not have
2 He likes restaurants, but he can't buy a
3 Today there are
4 He has an
5 There is
6 He can eat

a) meal today.
b) apple.
c) any money for food.
d) some bread in his cupboard.
e) some tomatoes in his fridge.
f) some tomato sandwiches and an apple today.

7 Complete the second sentence so that it means the same as the first. Use *some* or *any* + one word.

1 We don't have any water.

We need _some water_ .

2 We need some tomatoes.

We don't have _____.

3 I haven't got any vegetables.

I want _____.

4 There are no strawberries.

There aren't _____.

5 Do you sell oil?

Do you have _____?

6 No coffee for me, thank you.

I don't want _____, thank you.

7 I need some water, please.

Can you give me _____, please?

8 I want to ask you two or three questions. OK?

Can I ask you _____?

8 Read the text and answer the questions about the underlined words.

1 In paragraph 1, what does *It* mean?

_____

2 In paragraph 2, what does *This vitamin* mean?

_____

3 In paragraph 3, what does *this* mean?

_____

4 In paragraph 4, what does *these* mean?

_____

5 In the last sentence, what does *it* mean?

_____

9 Complete the summary about vitamin E.

VITAMIN E

Why important: _____

_____

In which foods: _____

_____

READING

READ BETTER

Look for signpost words in the text. They tell you what is coming next.

because introduces a reason.

such as and *for example* introduce examples.

also introduces similar information.

VITAMIN E

I The thing in this picture is not a flower. It is vitamin E. You need a good digital microscope to see it. Under the microscope, vitamin E is beautiful.

2 This vitamin is very important for our health, too. For example, it fights illness and is good for your heart. It is also good for your skin because it helps to repair the skin.

3 We get this vitamin from nuts and from green vegetables such as cabbage, broccoli and spinach. It is also in vegetable oil. We use this to cook food, and it has a lot of vitamin E. Avocado pears and brown bread have it, too.

4 You can also buy vitamins in bottles. There are two types of vitamin E in the shops: these are natural and man-made. The natural type is more expensive but it is better.

GRAMMAR: *much, many, a lot of*

1 Complete the conversation between a doctor and a patient with the words in the box.

a	an	any	~~much~~	many	a lot

D: How ¹ *much* fruit do you eat per week?

P: I eat ²_____ apple or
   ³_____ banana every day.

D: Good. Do you eat ⁴_____ vegetables?

P: I sometimes eat broccoli, but I don't eat
   ⁵_____ vegetables.

D: Do you eat ⁶_____ food in the
   mornings?

P: Yes, I have a big breakfast with bread and eggs.

D: How ⁷_____ eggs?

P: Two usually.

D: How ⁸_____ meat and fish do you
   eat?

P: I eat ⁹_____ of meat but I don't eat
   ¹⁰_____ fish.

D: OK. How ¹¹_____ cheese do you eat?

P: I always have ¹²_____ of cheese at
   lunch time.

D: You eat ¹³_____ of meat and cheese
   but not ¹⁴_____ vegetables. That's not
   good for you.

2 Write more questions for the doctor. Use these words and *How much or How many.*

1 coffee   *How much coffee do you drink?*

2 tea   _____

3 oranges   _____

3 Read the text and complete the questions and answers about it.

Scientists help farmers in dry countries >>>>>>
>>>>>>>>>>>>>>>>>>>>>

About 1.6 billion people live in dry countries. That is a quarter of the world's population, and the number is growing fast. In these countries, there is not much water for plants and animals. But scientists can help. They can now make new types of plant. These new plants do not need much water.

Water is not the only problem for farmers. Plants usually need a long time to grow. Scientists can help with this, too. For example, peas and beans usually need 180 days to grow, but now there is a new type of pea. Farmers can grow it in only 110 days.

1 Q: How _____?

   A: About 1.6 billion.

2 Q: Is there any water for plants and animals?

   A: Yes, there is, but _____.

3 Q: The new plants don't need any water, do they?

   A: Well, they need _____, but
      not much.

4 Q: _____ days do peas usually
      need to grow?

   A: About 180.

5 Q: _____ time do the new
      peas need?

   A: Only 110 days.

LISTENING

LISTEN BETTER

Read the questions *before* listening.
Guess possible words and phrases.
Listen for the answers.
Example: How many people are there in his family?
Possible words and phrases: *he has, he's got, there are, one, two, three, his wife, mother, father, brother(s) sister(s), children, boy, girl, son, daughter*

4 `30` Listen and answer these questions about the farmer in the picture.

1 How many people are there in his family? _____

2 How many months are wet? _____

3 How much TV does he watch? _____

4 Where does his son work? _____

PRONUNCIATION

5 `31` Can you hear pronunciation mistakes and correct pronunciation? Listen and write ✓ or ✗.

Sounds:

1 a) lives __✗__   b) lives __✓__

2 a) August _____   b) August _____

3 a) money _____   b) money _____

Word stress:

4 a) September _____   b) September _____

5 a) always _____   b) always _____

6 a) because _____   b) because _____

TRANSLATION

6 Translate into your language. Notice the differences.

1 Tomatoes are cheap but meat is expensive.

_____

2 We don't have much milk or many apples.

_____

3 I've got some bread but I haven't got any cheese.

_____

EXTRA VOCABULARY: how much food/drink?

7a Study these phrases.

A cup of coffee   A bottle of oil   A glass of water

A packet of crisps   A bag of sugar   A bar of chocolate

 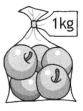 

A litre of fruit juice   A kilogram of apples   100 grams of cheese

7b Which word or phrase does NOT fit the gap? Cross it out.

1 A bottle of ... a) milk b) water c) ~~cheese~~ d) cola

2 A kilogram of ... a) meat b) rice c) carrots d) milk

3 A bag of ... a) potatoes b) water c) rice d) sugar

4 Two ... of tea
a) packets b) bars c) cups d) hundred grams

5 A glass of ...
a) crisps b) water c) milk d) apple juice

6 A litre of ...
a) oranges b) orange juice c) water d) milk

7 They eat a .... of chocolate every day.
a) cup b) bar c) kilo d) hundred grams

SPELLING

8 Add four words from Exercise 7 to each of the boxes in Exercise 3 on page 36.

VOCABULARY: food and drink

1 Which word does *not* fit the gap?

1 … course a) first b) main c) ~~apple~~ d) third

2 … curry
a) chicken b) beef c) vegetables d) vegetable

3 … salad a) fruit b) green c) tomato d) soup

4 … juice a) milk b) orange c) apple d) fruit

5 … soup
a) chicken b) tomato c) juice d) noodle

6 … water a) still b) sparkling c) cold d) dry

7 … food a) fast b) sparkling c) good d) English

2 Add these words to the boxes in Exercise 3 on page 36.

beef curry dessert Japan Morocco salad

KEY LANGUAGE: requests and offers

3a Choose the best sentence, a), b) or c), to complete the conversation.

1 A: I'm afraid we don't have any chicken.

   B: a) Have you got any?

      b) Thank you very much.

      c) Can we have some beef, then?

2 A: I'm hungry.

   B: a) Would you like an ice cream?

      b) Are you hungry?

      c) That's fine.

3 A: Do you have any apples?

   B: a) Not much.

      b) Yes. How many would you like?

      c) I'm sorry. I'm afraid we can't.

4 A: What would you like for your main course?

   B: a) A bottle of water, please.

      b) I'd like a chicken curry.

      c) Yes, I would.

5 A: I'm sorry. We haven't got any tomato soup.

   B: a) I'd like some, please.

      b) How much have you got?

      c) Can we have noodle soup?

6 A: Can we have 24 pizzas?

   B: a) That's no problem.

      b) Yes, please.

      c) No, thank you.

7 A: OK. What would you like?

   B: a) Could we have some apple pie, please?

      b) We haven't got any.

      c) Yes, please.

3b `32` Listen and check your answers.

4 Complete this email from a catering company to a conference organiser.

From… Julie Parsons
To… Kate Dawson
Subject: RE: Order

Dear Ms Dawson

Thank you for your order.

1_____ afraid we don't have any pistachio ice creams at the moment. We 2_____ provide strawberry, vanilla and 12 other types of ice cream.

Would 3_____ like still water or sparkling 4_____ with the meal?

Regards
Julie Parsons
Catering Manager

5 Complete the conference organiser's reply to the email in Exercise 4. Ask for chocolate ice creams (50) and sparkling water (20 bottles).

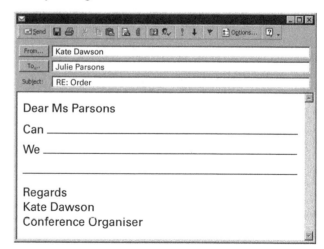

From… Kate Dawson
To… Julie Parsons
Subject: RE: Order

Dear Ms Parsons

Can _____

We _____

_____

Regards
Kate Dawson
Conference Organiser

STUDY SKILLS: correcting your writing

1 Cross out and correct the wrong prepositions. Tick the correct sentences.

1 We haven't got any ice cream ~~in~~ the moment. _at_

2 What would you like for lunch? ✓

3 Sardines are a kind of fish. _____

4 Vegetables are good of your health. _____

5 They are high on vitamin C. _____

6 The shop opens at eight at the morning. _____

7 In restaurants you pay for your food after the meal. _____

8 I usually go to the supermarket with car. _____

9 Cabbage is cheaper of broccoli. _____

10 I'd like to order food for 200 people. _____

2 A student listed some of his mistakes. Complete the corrections column for him.

Type of mistake	Mistakes	Corrections
Spelling	1 *sallad* 2 *Morroco* 3 *cabage* 4 *poeple* 5 *ilness*	1 _salad_ 2 _Morocco_ 3 _____ 4 _____ 5 _____
Grammar	6 *I no drink much tea.* 7 *Tea comes from the India.* 8 *How many tea would you like?*	6 _____ 7 _____ 8 _____
Wrong word	9 *I often <u>do</u> mistakes with grammar.* 10 *Can we have soup for the starter and beef for the main <u>meal</u>?* 11 *Can we have some green <u>vegetarians</u>, please?*	9 _____ 10 _____ 11 _____

WRITING SKILLS: a restaurant review

3a A review needs a good ending. Punctuate these endings correctly.

1 It has good food good music and cheap drinks so what are you waiting for

2 It is the best place in town for good cheap healthy food

3 Slow service dirty tables ugly pictures and bad food make this the worst restaurant in town

4 Its good its cheap and its friendly phone them now and eat there tonight

5 The food is not bad the drinks arent expensive and the music is good its a great place for a night out

3b Which ending do you like best?

DICTATION

4 33 Listen and write about the six best restaurants in the world. Use correct punctuation.

This is a picture of *Restaurant* magazine.

Every year this magazine makes a list of

_____

_____

_____

_____

_____

_____

_____

7 Shopping

7.1 CONSUMER HABITS

VOCABULARY: shopping

1 Complete the sentences with the verbs in the box. Write the verbs in the correct form.

| look at | ~~look for~~ | look for | pay for |
| spend ... on | think about | wait for | |

1 Can you help me, please? I'm *looking for* a new suit.

2 A: Can I help you?
   B: No, thanks. I'm just _____ a friend.

3 Can I _____ that digital camera, please?

4 I'm _____ buying some new shoes.

5 How would you like to _____ these shoes?

6 I don't _____ a lot of money _____ clothes.

7 I'm not _____ anything special; I'm just window shopping.

2 Look at the picture and complete the words in the gaps.

1 The young man is trying on a c_____.

2 He is wearing black sh_____.

3 The older man is wearing a grey s_____ and a white sh_____.

4 He is thinking about buying a pair of j_____.

GRAMMAR: present continuous (1)

3 Look at pictures 1–4 on page 43. What are the people doing? Use these phrases in the present continuous.

help a customer	look at cameras
window shop	think of buying a jacket
use her mobile	look for some new shoes

1 Helena *is thinking of buying a jacket.*

2 Pete _____

3 Maria and Sonia _____

4 Sonia _____

5 Philip _____

6 The customer in the shoe shop _____
_____

4 What are *you* doing now?

_____
_____

Look at another person. What is he/she doing?

_____
_____

5 Look at pictures 1–4 on page 43 and the information below. What work do the people do? Are they working now?

1 (Helena – hospital)

   Helena works in a hospital.

   She isn't working now.

2 (Pete – shoe shop)

   _____
   _____

3 (Maria and Sonia – university department)

   _____
   _____

4 (Philip – office)

   _____
   _____

LISTENING

6 [34] **Listen to three conversations and match them with three of the pictures.**

Conversation 1 = Picture _____

Conversation 2 = Picture _____

Conversation 3 = Picture _____

7a **Put the words in the right order to make sentences. Write C (Customer) or A (Assistant).**

1 you ? I help Can

thanks , No . just I'm looking .

_A_ : _Can I help you?_

_C_ : _____

2 need you Do help any ?

please , Yes . much these shoes are How ?

_A_ : _____

___ : _____

3 Can try on them I ?

course of Yes , .

___ : _____

___ : _____

4 size have you a larger Do ?

I'm don't we afraid but I can order you it for .

___ : _____

___ : _____

7b **Listen again and check your answers.**

TRANSLATION

8 Translate into your language. Notice the differences.

1 I can't talk now. I'm trying on some jeans.

_____

2 He isn't looking for anything. He's waiting for Tom.

_____

3 He always arrives late.

_____

4 Look! The bus is coming.

_____

VOCABULARY: shops and shopping

1 Choose the best word, a, b) or c), to complete the sentences.

1 You can use a computer for _online_ shopping.

a) window   b) online   c) town centre

2 Online booksellers can offer big _____.

a) discounts   b) prices   c) customers

3 Supermarkets sell many different _____.

a) hypermarkets   b) locations   c) products

4 Cafés and banks are examples of _____.

a) products   b) services   c) stores

5 Let's go _____.

a) shopping   b) buying   c) paying

6 This shop has lower _____.

a) food   b) products   c) prices

7 _____ like getting discounts.

a) Services   b) Customers   c) Products

GRAMMAR: present continuous (2)

2 Make questions with these words. Look at graphs 1 and 2 to answer the questions.

1 The number of small shops – grow?

Q: _Is the number of small food shops growing?_

A: _No, it isn't._

2 Mobile phone shops – do well?

Q: _____

A: _____

3 Bookshops – become more common?

Q: _____

A: _____

4 The price of cameras – go up or down?

Q: _____

A: _____

5 Houses – become cheaper or more expensive?

Q: _____

_____

A: _____

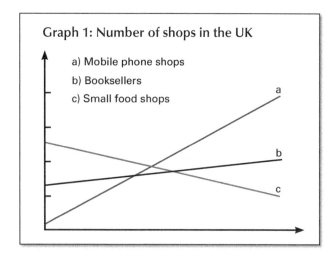

Graph 1: Number of shops in the UK

a) Mobile phone shops
b) Booksellers
c) Small food shops

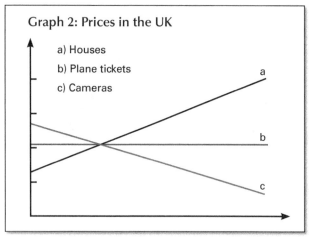

Graph 2: Prices in the UK

a) Houses
b) Plane tickets
c) Cameras

3 Read the information. Then ask for more information. Begin with the given word(s).

1 In the past, supermarkets sold just food. Now they are starting to sell other things.

What _other things are they starting to sell?_

2 Some shops are not doing well.

Which _____

3 Tesco is building new stores.

Where _____

4 The company is opening a lot of new shops.

How many _____

5 The company is making a lot of money.

How much _____

6 Town centres are changing.

How _____

7 Travel is becoming more popular.

Why _____

READING

READ BETTER

We sometimes want to find just one or two items of information in a text, so we **scan** the text for that information. Practise scanning in Exercise 4.

4 Scan the text about pop-up stores for answers to these questions. <u>Underline</u> the answers in the text. You have one minute.

1 What are pop-up stores?

2 Find five examples of pop-up stores.

5 Now read the text about pop-up stores and answer the questions with *Yes* or *No*.

1 Is 'pop-up store' an old word? *no*

2 Are pop-up stores popular?

3 Are pop-up stores usually expensive?

4 Does the London Fashion Bus sell clothes?

5 Are any big companies opening pop-up stores?

SPELLING: adding -ing

6 Read the rules. Then add **-ing** to verbs 1–10.

Verbs ending in -e: Delete the *e* before adding *-ing*.
change → changing

Verbs ending in -ie: Change *ie* to *y*.
die → dying

Verbs ending in only one *stressed* vowel + only one consonant: Double the consonant.
*get → ge**tt**ing; begin → begi**nn**ing*

All other verbs: Add *-ing*.
*study → studying; spend → spending;
open → opening; cook → cooking*

1 go *going*

2 try _____

3 use _____

4 look _____

5 put _____

6 make _____

7 lie _____

8 visit _____

9 stay _____

10 shop _____

HOME NEWS SPORT COMMENT MONEY TRAVEL

Pop-up stores are coming to a street near you!

The name 'pop-up store' is only a few years old, but it is becoming more common because the number of pop-up stores is growing in cities all over the world.

Pop-up stores are a type of shop. They open for a short time – between a week and a year – and then close down or move to a new place.

An example is the US fashion company, Vacant. Their store sells clothes by famous designers and new designers. The store opens for just one month in a big city like New York, Tokyo, Shanghai, Paris, Berlin, Stockholm or Los Angeles, then it closes down and moves. The advantages? The shop is always new and interesting, so it gets a lot of customers. Another advantage is that the store uses an empty building in a cheap part of the city, so it saves money and it can offer good prices.

The London Fashion Bus is another example. It is a big bus, which stops for a week in different places and brings exciting London fashions to other parts of the UK.

Pop-up stores are doing well, and now bigger companies, like Amazon, JC Penny and Nike, are starting to open pop-up stores. They are probably coming to a street near you!

KEY LANGUAGE: giving advantages and disadvantages

1a Complete the discussion in a business studies class between some students and the teacher.

T: A lot of people think traditional shopping is dying. Well, online shopping [1] _has_ a lot of advantages, but does it have any disadvantages?

S1: Yes, it does. I think there are two [2] _____ disadvantages. The first is that you can't see the real products. This [3] _____ that you can't try on clothes or check that food is good, for example.

T: Right. What's the second disadvantage?

S1: Well, the second is [4] _____ you order a product online and then you wait for a few days – or weeks. In a shop, you can get the product right there.

T: Good. What other advantages [5] _____ traditional shopping [6] _____?

S2: One important advantage [7] _____ [8] _____ a lot of people enjoy traditional shopping. I don't think online shopping can change that.

S3: Yes, and [9] _____ advantage is that it's good for you. I mean it's healthier than sitting at a computer.

T: OK. Are there any [10] _____ advantages?

1b 〔35〕 Listen and check your answers.

PRONUNCIATION: stressed words

2a Look at the words in *italics*. Underline the stressed word.

1 A: Are there any disadvantages?
  B: There are _two_ disadvantages.

2 A: The first disadvantage is that you can't see the products.
  B: What's _the second_ disadvantage?

3 A: I like online shopping.
  B: What about _traditional shopping_?

4 A: What advantage does traditional shopping have?
  B: I think people _enjoy it_.

5 A: Who thinks online shopping is better?
  B: _I_ think online shopping _is_ better.

6 A: Online shopping is quicker and cheaper.
  B: Are _there_ any _more_ advantages?

2b 〔36〕 Listen and check your answers.

VOCABULARY: American and British English

3 Translate this paragraph about an American town into British English.

From the highway, it's just a five-minute drive to the downtown area. There you find a small but busy shopping mall with good stores and some nice cafés. Parking is no problem because there is a big parking lot, and there is a gas station near the highway.

From the main road, it's _____

_____

_____

_____

_____

_____

_____

_____

_____

_____

STUDY SKILLS: giving a short, informal talk

1 `37` Listen to the talk about emails and complete the notes.

Emails

Addresses: @ = at
           . = dot

Greetings: ¹ _Hi_ + name (informal)

        ² _____ + name

Some opening phrases

  How ³ _____?

  How are ⁴ _____? (USA)

  I hope ⁵ _____ well.

  Thank ⁶ _____ your message.

Some common endings

  for family:

    ⁷ _____ or ⁸ _____

  for friends or family:

    Bye for now or ⁹ _____

  for friends or informal business:

    ¹⁰ _____ wishes or

    ¹¹ _____

DICTATION: email addresses

2 `38` Listen and write the email addresses.

1 _jones@tbn.co.uk_

2 _____

3 _____

4 _____

5 _____

WRITING SKILLS: an email

3 Choose the best word or phrase, a), b) or c), to complete the emails.

An email from a student to another student.

> ¹ _____ Ali
>
> ² _____ things? Your mobile phone isn't working. Do you have my Chemistry book? I can't find it.
>
> Bye ³ _____
>
> Vasil

1 a) Hi   b) The   c) How

2 a) Hello   b) How are   c) I hope

3 a) for now   b) Take care   c) you later

An email from a student to a lecturer

> ⁴ _____ Dr Jones
>
> Thank ⁵ _____ message. I am trying to decide about my course for next semester. Can I talk to you about it?
>
> ⁶ _____
>
> Vasil Turgut

4 a) Hi   b) Dear   c) Sorry

5 a) you for   b) your for you   c) you for your

6 a) Best wishes   b) Love   c) See you soon

4 Complete the sentences with the words in the box.

> ~~and~~   because (x2)   but   or   so (x2)

1 I buy a lot of books _and_ I borrow a lot of books.

2 I like funny stories _____ I don't like sad stories.

3 Do you like novels _____ do you prefer fact books?

4 I bought this for Paula _____ it's her birthday.

5 I want to remember this information _____ I'm writing notes.

6 I'm writing to you _____ I can't find your phone number.

7 It's important _____ don't forget it.

8 History and culture

8.1 PAST TIMES

VOCABULARY: buildings

1 Write the words in the box under the correct heading. (Some words can go under more than one heading.)

> courtyard   door   entrance   furniture
> garden   gate   ladder   painting   roof
> room   wall   window

Inside a house	Between inside and outside	Outside a house
door	*door*	*courtyard*

GRAMMAR: past simple of *to be*

2 Complete the text about an old Roman city with *was, wasn't, were, weren't, is* or *are*.

This is Leptis Magna in modern-day Libya, North Africa. It was an important city from about 1000 BC. After 200 BC it was part of the Roman Empire and it ¹ *was* one of the biggest cities in Africa. In those days, North Africa ² _____ greener than it is now. There was always a lot of rain, but then there was a change in the climate about 2,000 years ago. After that, the weather ³ _____ dryer. There ⁴ _____ much rain, and the land wasn't green; it was sandy desert. In about 650 AD, parts of the city ⁵ _____ under sand because sand in North Africa moves all the time. After that, there ⁶ _____ any people in the city. Some time later, all of the city was under sand. It ⁷ _____ under the sand for 1,200 years but now we can see it again, thanks to the work of archaeologists. It isn't the only Roman city in the world today (there ⁸ _____ others in Italy, for example), but it ⁹ _____ one of the most interesting.

3 Complete questions for these answers about the city in Exercise 2 on page 48.

1 Q: _Where is_ Leptis Magna?
A: It's in Libya, North Africa.

2 Q: How _____ Leptis Magna?
A: It's about 3,000 years old.

3 Q: When _____ in the Roman Empire?
A: After 200 BC.

4 Q: _____ a change in the climate?
A: Yes, there was.

5 Q: _____ parts of the city under sand?
A: In about 650 AD.

6 Q: How _____ the city under sand?
A: For about 1,200 years.

7 Q: _____ any other Roman cities?
A: Yes, there are, especially in Italy.

4 Which word or phrase does _not_ fit the gap? Cross it out.

1 He was here last ... .
a) year   b) month   c) week   d) ~~day~~

2 The shop is open ... .
a) today   b) yesterday   c) now   d) on Sundays

3 His last school exam was in ... .
a) June   b) the summer   c) Monday   d) 2000

4 I was there on ... .
a) Sunday   b) July   c) 1 May   d) National Day

5 The museum closes at ... .
a) 5 p.m.   b) the weekend   c) Christmas   d) August

6 They were here ... ago.
a) last week   b) 10 minutes   c) a week   d) 1,000 years

7 I was there last ... .
a) night   b) hour   c) weekend   d) week

LISTENING

LISTEN BETTER

In talks and lectures, speakers often ...

1 say what the talk is about.

2 ask a question and then answer it.

3 use 'signpost' words like _First_ and _For example_.

4 give information.

5 give examples.

5 〔39〕 Look at the _Listen better_ box and listen to a lecture. Tick the things in the box (1–5) the lecturer does.

6 Listen again and complete the information about Roman civilisation.

1 Period of civilisation: _about 500 BC to 476 AD_

2 Main period: _____

3 Location: southern Europe,

_____,

the eastern Mediterranean,

and parts of _____

4 Capital city: _____

5 Good at a) _____

b) _____

c) _____

d) _____

SPELLING: similar words

7 Underline the correct word.

1 The Romans _wear/were/where/we're_ good at building roads.

2 _Their/There/They're_ communication systems were good.

3 Chinese civilisation is older _that/then/than_ Western civilisation.

4 Indian films are _quite/quiet_ popular in Europe now.

5 Russia is a very big country. _It's/Its_ capital is Moscow.

6 We sometimes _wash/watch_ TV in the _kitchen/chicken_.

DICTATION

8 〔40〕 Listen and write the sentences.

1 _____

2 _____
_____

3 _____
_____

4 _____
_____

THEN AND NOW

GRAMMAR: *could, couldn't*

1 Complete the sentences about famous people with *can*, *can't*, *could* or *couldn't*.

A Mozart, one of the world's most famous musicians, [1] *could* play the piano well when he was five years old.

B Ricky Molier is a famous tennis player.
He [2]_____ walk but he
[3]_____ hit the ball at 160kph.

C Einstein, the world's most famous scientist, was a slow learner when he was young.
He [4]_____ read until he was nine.

D Shakespeare (1564–1616), the world's most famous writer, [5]_____ decide how to spell his name: was it Shakespeare, Shaksper or Shakespere? We spell his name Shakespeare now, but we [6]_____ be sure how to pronounce it correctly.

E One of the world's best linguists was Georges Schmidt (1915–90), a translator at the UN. He [7]_____ translate 66 languages, but he [8]_____ speak 'only' 19 of them well. He [9]_____ find time to practise the other 47.

2 Complete the sentences about *you*.

1 When I was _____, I could _____

_____

   but I couldn't _____

2 When I was _____, I _____

   but I _____

VOCABULARY: verbs + prepositions

3a Which verbs can go with these phrases? Complete the puzzle.

1 ... to friends on the phone
2 ... for a train at a station
3 ... onto the next topic
4 ... about buying some new shoes
5 ... to your teacher about a problem
6 ... with your left hand
7 ... on the most important questions
8 ... about interesting things in books
9 ... in a hotel
10 ... to music
11 ... on a trip
12 ... money on clothes

1			c	h	a	t	

3b What is the mystery word?

READING

4a Read the article about technology and culture.

Technology and culture

Changes in technology bring changes in culture. A good example is the car.

A suburb in the USA in the 1940s

Before cars and buses, most people couldn't live far from their work, so there were two types of people: town people and country people, with two different cultures. But in the 1900s, town workers could get the bus or drive to work. So people started to live in new suburbs (areas *between* the town and the country). Life in the suburbs was different from town life and country life, so a new culture grew up – suburban culture.

Cars changed town culture, too. Before cars and buses, walking was the main way of getting around, and most people never went far from their homes. So people often saw their neighbours in the street. Most people knew every family in their street and could name every person. Cars changed that. Now, for the first time in history, most of us do not know the people in our street.

4b Read these sentences about the article. Say if they are true, false or the article doesn't say.

1 Before cars and buses, most people's homes were near their work. *true*

2 In the 1900s, workers could only walk or cycle to work.

3 About 50% of town workers live in suburbs.

4 People were healthier and fitter before the 1900s.

5 Before cars, most people didn't know many other people.

6 Most people now can't name all the people in their street.

7 Our culture is different now because of cars.

8 The writer thinks the changes are bad.

PRONUNCIATION: /tʃ/, /k/, /ʃ/

5 Match these words with the consonant sounds. Check in your dictionary.

<u>ch</u>ange cul<u>t</u>ure e<u>c</u>onomi<u>c</u>s informa<u>t</u>ion ma<u>ch</u>ine ma<u>k</u>e <u>sh</u>op te<u>ch</u>nology wa<u>tch</u>

1 /tʃ/ *change* _____

2 /k/ _____

3 /ʃ/ _____

6 Which sound is different from the other two? Cross it out. Check in your dictionary.

1 a) tea<u>ch</u>er   b) whi<u>ch</u>   c) ~~<u>ch</u>emistry~~

2 a) furni<u>t</u>ure   b) <u>ch</u>ocolate   c) popula<u>t</u>ion

3 a) mu<u>ch</u>   b) Engli<u>sh</u>   c) <u>Ch</u>icago

4 a) ma<u>tch</u>   b) <u>ch</u>at   c) s<u>ch</u>ool

KEY LANGUAGE: polite requests

1 Change these questions and instructions into polite requests. Use *Could you ..., please?*.

1 Open the door.

   Could you open the door, please?

2 Where is the café?

   Could you tell me where the café is, please?

3 Help me.

   _____

4 Show me the way out.

   _____

5 Where are the lifts?

   _____

6 How much is this map?

   _____

7 What time does the museum open?

   _____

8 What does this notice mean?

   _____

2 ▣41 Listen and choose the best response, a) or b).

1 a) I'm afraid not, sir.

   b) Yes, sir. How can I help you?

2 a) Let me see. That's £70.

   b) What would you like?

3 a) I'm afraid not.

   b) I'm afraid I can't do that.

4 a) Sure. No problem.

   b) Can I help you?

5 a) I'm afraid not, sir, but you can leave them here.

   b) That's no problem, sir. You can leave them here.

6 a) Not at all, sir.

   b) Yes, sir.

7 a) Yes, of course. Here you are.

   b) Not at all. Here you are.

8 a) Yes, of course, madam. It's £6.

   b) Yes, madam. Go through that door and turn left.

9 a) You're welcome.

   b) Certainly.

VOCABULARY: words from the lesson

3 Write the jumbled words correctly.

1 sumeum <u>m u s e u m</u>

2 tographoph <u>p h</u> _ _ _ _ _ _ _ _

3 coaklmoor <u>c l</u> _ _ _ _ _ _ _

4 rastis <u>s t</u> _ _ _ _ _

5 kictet <u>t</u> _ _ _ _ _ _

6 hibextioni <u>e</u> _ _ _ _ _ _ _ _ _

EXTRA VOCABULARY: prepositions of movement

4 Match the <u>underlined</u> prepositions 1–9 with the diagrams a–h. Check in your dictionary.

1 Go <u>across</u> the street. <u>h</u>

2 Go <u>through</u> the entrance to the main hall. _____

3 Go <u>to</u> the desk and buy your ticket. _____

4 Walk <u>towards</u> the stairs. _____

5 Go <u>down</u> to the cloakroom and leave your coat. _____

6 Then take the lift <u>up</u> to the third floor. _____

7 Go <u>out of</u> the lift. _____

8 Walk <u>along</u> the corridor. _____

9 Go <u>into</u> the big room. _____

a) →→ ☐   f) ↓

b) →→|☐| g)

c) →→|☐| h)

d) |→→| i)

e) ↑

STUDY SKILLS: learning new words

1 Use the clues to complete the words. Be careful with spelling.

Shapes

1 _t r i a n g l e_

2  _r_ _ _ _ _ _ _ _ _

3 _s_ _ _ _ _

4 _c_ _ _ _ _ _

Materials

5  _m_ _ _ _ _

6  _l_ _ _ _ _ _ _

7  _p_ _ _ _ _ _ _

2 Complete the sentences with the word in brackets in the correct form.

1 What is the _length_ (long) of this car?

2 How much does this _____ (weigh)?

3 What is the _____ (wide) of the road?

4 It's a _____ (circle) table.

5 Most pictures are _____ (rectangle).

6 What are those men doing? They are _____ (wide) the road.

7 Can you _____ (long) these trousers?

8 The computer has a _____ (weigh) of only 2 kilograms.

WRITING SKILLS: a description of an object

3 Rewrite this description with correct punctuation and capital letters.

this beautiful plate is from iraq and is more than 1100 years old the colours are white blue and brown the circle of shapes in the middle includes triangles half circles and flower shapes the big blue squares outside this circle are unusual the plate is in excellent condition

_____

_____

_____

_____

_____

_____

_____

_____

_____

_____

_____

TRANSLATION

4 Translate into your language. Notice the differences.

1 There weren't many people here today.

_____

2 She couldn't carry it.

_____

3 Could you tell me when the next film starts?

_____

9 Inventions

9.1 MARVELLOUS MINDS

1 Complete the sentences with the verbs in the box in the past simple.

enjoy	finish	help	start
stay	~~visit~~	want	return

We ¹ _visited_ my cousins last weekend because they

² _____ to show us their new house.

My uncle ³ _____ to build the house two

years ago and he ⁴ _____ it last month.

I ⁵ _____ the trip very much.

We ⁶ _____ there for two days.

I ⁷ _____ with some work in the garden.

Finally, we ⁸ _____ home.

2 Write the present tense verbs in the box in alphabetical order. Then write the past simple forms. Check your answers in your Coursebook (see page 159).

go	have	write	~~come~~	sell
~~build~~	make	~~drive~~	get	see

	Present	Past simple
1	build	built
2	come	
3	drive	
4		
5		
6		
7		
8		
9		
10		

3 Choose the correct form of the verbs to complete the sentences.

1 We ᵃ⁾*live/lives/lived* in London when I was younger, but we ᵇ⁾*move/moves/moved* last year and now we ᶜ⁾*live/lives/lived* in Oxford.

2 I never ᵃ⁾*play/plays/played* football now, but I often ᵇ⁾*play/plays/played* when I was younger.

3 Ali ᵃ⁾*study/studies/studied* Chemistry at university. After that, he ᵇ⁾*go/goes/went* to a university in England. Now he ᶜ⁾*work/works/worked* for an oil company.

4 Anita ᵃ⁾*start/starts/started* a small company in 1995. It ᵇ⁾*produce/produces/produced* women's clothes. In 2000 it ᶜ⁾*become/becomes/became* very successful. Last year, she ᵈ⁾*sell/sells/sold* the company. Now she ᵉ⁾*have/has/had* a new business.

4 Complete the second sentence so that it means the same as the first. Use **when** + the verb **be**.

1 He started work at the age of 16.

He started work _when he was 16_ .

2 They met at university.

They met _____ at university.

3 As a teenager, she played basketball.

_____ teenager, she played basketball.

4 I was 22. I left university.

_____ I left university.

5 He was only 30. He became a professor.

He became a professor _____ .

6 I was in London and I saw the Queen.

I saw the Queen _____ .

7 He started his first business at the age of 24.

He started his first business _____ .

5 Complete the sentences with the correct form of the verbs in the box. Check your answers in your Coursebook (see page 159).

| buy hear know read teach spend |

1 I *bought* some clothes last weekend.

2 I _____ my little brother to swim last year.

3 I _____ a good book last week.

4 I _____ a lot of money yesterday.

5 I _____ him a long time ago.

6 I _____ a lot of noise last night.

LISTENING

6 [42] Study the pictures. Then listen and complete the notes.

Thomas Edison

A telegraph in the 1860s

A phonograph

Edison's light bulb

1 *1854* 7 years old; spent a few months at school

2 _____ started work when 13, selling newspapers

1862–69 worked as a telegraph operator

1869 invented a better telegraph printer and got 3$_____

4 _____ built a laboratory

5 _____ invented a recording machine (a phonograph)

6 _____ invented an electric light bulb

7 _____ started companies to produce lighting systems

8 _____ produced some of the first moving pictures

By 1915 his laboratories employed 9_____ people

10 _____ died

SPELLING: long words

7 Match the parts to make long words.

1	~~hel~~	gin	tri	ing	
2	en	vent	~~cop~~	ar	ty
3	e	~~i~~	ul	at	ion
4	rec	lec	ci	ci	
5	in	nun	ion	~~ter~~	
6	pro	tang	eer		

1 *helicopter*   4 _____

2 _____   5 _____

3 _____   6 _____

DICTATION

8 [43] Listen and write the words.

1 _____

2 _____

3 _____

4 _____

5 _____

6 _____

VOCABULARY: the body

1 Complete the words. Check in your dictionary.

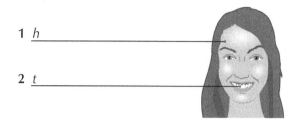

1 *h* _____

2 *t* _____

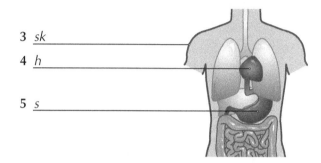

3 *sk* _____
4 *h* _____

5 *s* _____

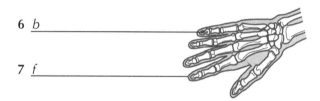

6 *b* _____

7 *f* _____

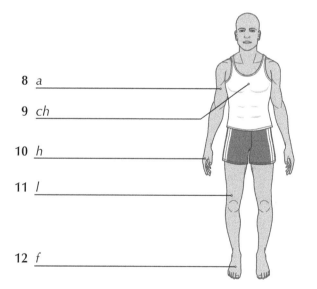

8 *a* _____

9 *ch* _____

10 *h* _____

11 *l* _____

12 *f* _____

GRAMMAR: past simple (negative)

2 Complete the sentences with the past form of the verb in brackets.

1 When I was in England, I *broke* (break) a bone.

2 I _____ (can not) walk.

3 A friend _____ (take) me to hospital.

4 We _____ (not know) much English.

5 The doctor _____ (not speak) my language.

6 The people at the hospital _____ (be) nice.

7 But I _____ (not enjoy) the experience!

8 I _____ (not need) to stay in the hospital.

9 I _____ (go) home the same day.

3 Choose the best word or phrase, a), b) or c), to complete the sentences.

1 When did _____ acupuncture?
a) they invent b) they invented c) invented

2 When _____ first go abroad?
a) you did b) you c) did you

3 Did you _____?
a) enjoyed it b) it enjoy c) enjoy it

4 Yes, I _____.
a) enjoyed b) did c) enjoy it

5 What _____ at the weekend?
a) you did b) did you c) did you do

6 I _____ well yesterday.
a) not feel b) didn't feel c) feel not

7 _____ to the doctor?
a) Did you go b) Did you c) You go

8 No, _____.
a) I didn't b) I go c) I went

9 _____ Thomas Edison invent?
a) What b) What did he c) What did

10 Who _____ at the hospital?
a) you saw b) see you c) did you see

TRANSLATION

4 Translate into your language. Notice the differences.

1 What did you say?

_____

2 Did you like it?

_____

3 Jansen invented the microscope.

_____

4 Hospitals didn't have scanners before the 1980s.

_____

_____

READING

5 Look at the pictures. Which invention is ...

1 for people who need eye drops?

2 for people with wet noses?

3 for people who often lose umbrellas?

6 Read the information below. Then match four of the paragraphs with the items a–d.

READ BETTER

Always think: '*What is this paragraph doing?*'
Is it ...

a) giving examples? _____

b) introducing a topic? _1_

c) giving reasons or opinions? _____

d) defining? _____

7 Read the article about chindogu and write one-word answers.

1 What is the name of this type of invention?

  chindogu

2 Do these inventors want to make money?

  _____

3 In which country did chindogu start?

  _____

4 When did it become popular outside Japan?

  _____

5 Was the first chindogu book successful?

  _____

6 Can the writer say why chindogu is popular?

  _____

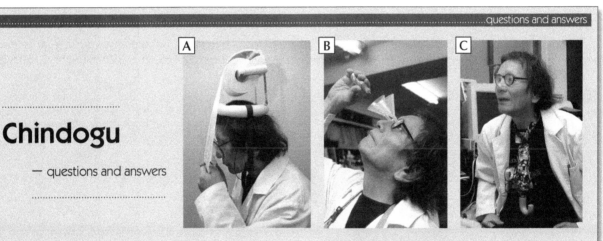

....questions and answers

Chindogu

— questions and answers

1 Chindogu is becoming more popular around the world.

2 **What is chindogu?**
Chindogu is a type of invention. The word comes from Japanese.

3 **What is the difference between chindogu and other inventions?**
Normal inventors hope to make money from their inventions. Chindogu inventors do not. They invent because they enjoy it. Normal inventors try to invent useful things. Chindogu inventors try to invent things that are almost useful. Their inventions are somewhere between useful and useless.

4   Examples include an umbrella tie, eye-drop glasses for people with eye problems, and an all-day tissue dispenser for people with colds.

Where and when did chindogu begin? **5**
Chindogu started in Japan in the 1980s and became world-famous in the 1990s.

How did it become popular? **6**
In the 1990s, a Japanese inventor wrote a book about chindogu. Millions of people bought his book. Now there are chindogu books in many languages, chindogu websites on the Internet and thousands of chindogu inventors.

Why did it become popular? **7**
This is a difficult question to answer. Chindogu inventions are usually funny. But they are more than just funny. They are ... Maybe we need to invent a new word to describe them!

questions and answers...

1 Complete the answer to the questions. Use the word *reason*.

1 'I'm sorry I didn't finish the work in time. I wasn't well last night and I couldn't find my dictionary.'

Q: Why didn't he finish the work in time?

A: One *reason is that he wasn't well.*

Another _____

_____

2 Jansen invented a microscope in about 1590, but people didn't think it was useful. Also, it didn't give a very clear picture.

Q: Why weren't people very interested in this invention?

A: The main _____

_____

The second _____

_____

2 44 Listen and answer the questions in the same way as in Exercise 1.

1 Q: Why did cars become more popular in the 1920s?

A: One _____

_____

_____

_____

2 Q: Why is Thomas Edison one of the most famous inventors?

A: The first _____

_____

_____

_____

_____

The	advantage/disadvantage	is that ...
	problem	
	important/interesting/funny thing	
	good/bad news	
	difference (between x and y)	
	answer	
	truth	

3 Choose the best words to complete the sentences.

1 Q: How was your exam yesterday?

A: Well the *good/bad* news is that Part 1 was easy, but the *good/bad* news is that I didn't finish Part 2.

2 The *difference/advantage* between 'color' and 'colour' is *that/than* 'color' is the American spelling and 'colour' is British.

3 I'd like to visit England, but the *answer/problem* is that it's expensive.

4 Q: Why is English spelling so irregular?

A: That's a good question. I think the *difference/answer* is that English words come from many different languages with different spelling systems.

4 45 Listen and write the words under the correct heading. Underline the stressed syllables.

~~called~~ ~~dangerous~~ European experiment looked microscope needed population started umbrella wanted worked

one syllable	two syllables	three syllables	four syllables
called		*dangerous*	

STUDY SKILLS: taking notes

1 Read about abbreviations and complete the examples below.

> We often use symbols and abbreviations to write notes.
> Examples:
> + = and   b = born
> c = century   d = died
> max = maximum   temp = temperature

Two ways of making abbreviations:

1) Use the first letter only

century → c

United Nations → UN

kilometres per hour → _____

United States → _____

2) Use the first part of a word

information → info

technology → tech

College → Col

company → _____

WRITING SKILLS: short biographies

2 Complete the texts about women inventors with the words in the box.

> after   at that time   ~~before~~
> during   earlier   later   then

Windscreen wipers

[1] *Before* 1903, cars did not have any windscreen wipers. [2]_____ bad weather, drivers couldn't see through their windscreens.
[3]_____ in 1903, an American woman, Mary Anderson, invented windscreen wipers. A short time [4]_____, all American cars had wipers. [5]_____ that, another woman, Charlotte Bridgwood, invented electric wipers in 1917.

>> Gertrude Elion

Gertrude Elion was an important 20th century scientist who received the Nobel Prize for Medicine in 1988. She was born 70 years [6]_____ in 1918 in the United States. When she was 15, her grandfather died of cancer. [7]_____, there were not many cancer-fighting drugs. Gertrude wanted to change that so she studied Chemistry at Hunter College and got her Master of Science (MS) degree at New York University. [8]_____ university, she got a job with a medical company. [9]_____ her working life, she invented an important cancer-fighting drug and many other life-saving drugs. She died in 1999.

3 Complete these notes about Gertrude Elion. Use abbreviations from Exercise 1.

> Gertrude Elion
> - Important 20th [1] _c_ scientist
> - [2]_____ 1918 in [3]_____
> - Grandfather [4]_____ cancer
> - Studied Chem at Hunter [5]_____
> - Got [6]_____ at New York Univ
> - Job with medical [7]_____
> - Invented cancer drug [8]_____ many others
> - Nobel Prize 1988
> - [9]_____ 1999

10.1 KEEPING IT SAFE

VOCABULARY: money

1 Choose the best word or phrase, a), b) or c), to complete the advertisement for a credit card.

ABC
Personal Banking

Put our card in your [1] _wallet_.

Cash is bad for you! [2]_____ are heavy and bad for your clothes. Carrying lots of [3]_____ can be dangerous. But don't worry! Just carry a [4]_____ or debit card from ABC Bank. Say goodbye to big [5]_____ and wallets and leave the [6]_____ book at home. When you need cash, you can get it from a [7]_____ easily.

Remember: don't tell anyone your [8]_____.

1 a) number   b) wallet   c) mobile

2 a) Coins   b) Notes   c) Money

3 a) pieces of paper   b) notes   c) cashpoints

4 a) PIN number   b) cashpoint   c) credit card

5 a) taxis   b) managers   c) purses

6 a) cheque   b) Chemistry   c) cheap

7 a) cashpoint   b) sports club   c) computer

8 a) card number   b) PIN number
   c) cheque number

GRAMMAR: should, shouldn't

2 Complete the information for international students studying in the UK. Use *should* or *shouldn't* with these words:

1 You   have

2 I   bring

3 you   carry

4 you   bring

5 I   get

6 you   get

7 you   have

8 I   do

9 you   apply

student support services
studying in the uk   SSS

Advice about money

The following information answers some of the questions that international students often ask.

How much money do I need for living expenses?

[1] _You should have_ about £8,000 or more per year for things like accommodation, food, clothes, books, travel and entertainment.

How much cash [2]_____?

Traveller's cheques are safer than cash, so [3]_____ a lot of cash. However, [4]_____ some cash for transport from the airport and for the first few days in the UK.

[5]_____ a UK credit card?

For a course of more than 6 months, [6]_____ a UK debit card. This is cheaper than using a foreign card. A credit card can be useful, too, but be careful about credit cards: they can get you into debt so [7]_____ more than one.

What [8]_____ to get help?

You can apply for help from your government or from the British Council in your country, but [9]_____ a year or more before your course starts.

decision making funding
money jobs career
career choice jobs decisions
applications

READING

3a Read the advice about student jobs.

student support services

studying in the uk | SSS

Advice about student jobs

Most international students on long courses in the UK can work during the holidays and up to a maximum of 20 hours per week during terms.

You need a National Insurance number (NI number) to work in the UK. You should apply for this before you start work but you can start work before your number arrives.

Most universities advise that students shouldn't work more than 15 hours a week in terms, so many students do part-time jobs, especially in restaurants or bars in the evenings or in shops at weekends.

In the holidays, full-time jobs are possible. Remember that a lot of students are looking for jobs at these times so you should start looking early.

Where and how should you look for jobs? The university careers office or job shop has information about jobs on and off the campus. You should also look at notices on other noticeboards in your university. Look for signs in the windows of shops and restaurants, too. Recruitment agencies, local newspapers and websites are also good places to look. And don't forget you can just ask local employers. You should talk to other students and ask their advice, too.

decision making   **career**   decisions
vacancies jobs
applications **jobs** career choice

3b Complete the notes about the advice.

International students on long courses:

- Can work in hols
- In terms – max [1] _20_ hrs per week
- Need [2] _____ number

Term jobs:

Universities advise max [3] _____ hrs per week.

e.g. restaurants, bars, [4] _____

Where to look for holiday jobs:

- Univ careers office / job shop
- Other [5] _____
- [6] _____
- Recruitment [7] _____
- Local [8] _____
- Websites
- Local [9] _____

VOCABULARY: words from the lesson

4 Underline the best word to complete the sentences.

1 How do you want to pay: credit card or *money/cash*?

2 The company makes a lot of *money/cash*.

3 I can't *afford/pay* to buy expensive clothes.

4 My parents pay the university *fees/courses*.

5 I often use my credit card and now I'm in *debt/debit*.

6 Someone *steal/stole* my debit card yesterday.

7 He *lost/found* his wallet, so he needs a new card.

SPELLING: *ant, ent, int*

5 Complete these words with *ant, ent* or *int*.

1 stud _e_ _n_ _t_   7 travel ag __ __ __

2 cashpo __ __ __   8 differ __ __ __

3 governm __ __ __   9 __ __ __ eresting

4 account __ __ __   10 sci __ __ __ ist

5 __ __ __ ernational   11 statem __ __ __

6 restaur __ __ __   12 import __ __ __

VOCABULARY:
phrases connected with money

1 Complete the conversation between two friends with the phrases in the box.

> borrow some cash
> borrowed £10
> charges interest
> earn money
> get a loan
> lend me £20
> pay me back
> ~~spent a lot of money~~

A: I [1] *spent a lot of money* yesterday so I need to [2] _____ from you.

B: Did you say 'borrow some cash'?

A: Yes. Can you [3] _____?

B: You [4] _____ from me last week.

A: I know, but I'm a student and you've got a job and you [5] _____.

B: When can you [6] _____?

A: I don't know.

B: Maybe you should [7] _____ from the bank.

A: But the bank [8] _____ at 15%.

B: So I'm cheaper than the bank!

GRAMMAR:
have to, don't have to

2 Match the signs and notices a–e with the sentences 1–8.

1 You have to drive slowly.   *c*

2 Most people have to pay to go in.

3 You don't have to drive slowly.

4 Very young people don't have to pay.

5 Small children can't go in without paying.

6 A teenager doesn't have to go with an older person but a younger child does.

7 You can't use a camera inside.

8 Students don't have to pay anything now.

a)

> Museum entrance fees
> Adults £5.00
> Students £4.00
> Children under 5 ....Free
> No photography

b)

c)

d)

> **STUDENTS!**
> Open a bank account and borrow £500 interest free. No interest for four years!

e)

> **Swimming pool**
> £4.00 per person
> No children under 12 without an adult

3 Complete the questions about working in a bank. Use *have to* and the words in brackets.

1 *Do you have to work* on Saturdays? (you   work)

2 _____ a uniform? (you   wear)

3 _____ a university degree? (you   have)

4 _____ good at Maths? (you   be)

5 What time _____ there in the morning? (you   be)

6 What time _____ there? (the bank manager   get)

4 Complete the sentences with the correct form of *(not) have to* + a verb.

1 A bank manager *doesn't have to work* at weekends.

2 A bank manager _____ a uniform.

3 A bank manager _____ good qualifications.

4 Students _____ careful with money.

5 With a credit card, you _____ a lot of cash.

TRANSLATION

5 Translate into your language. Notice the differences.

1 You shouldn't carry a lot of cash.

_____

2 You don't have to work at weekends.

_____

3 Do we have to finish this today?

_____

4 Bank managers have to have qualifications.

_____

LISTENING

LISTEN BETTER

There are three types of listening.

1 We sometimes need to understand just the **main ideas.**
   e.g. opinions in a conversation

2 We sometimes want just **a few details.**
   e.g. names or numbers

3 We sometimes want to understand **100%.**
   e.g. in a science lecture at university

Always think, '_Why am I listening? Is it type 1, 2 or 3?_'

6 46 **Listen for the main ideas in this conversation. Choose the best summary, a) or b).**

a) British students have to pay university fees and they can't always get loans. The American thinks the fees are expensive.

b) British students can get loans for university fees. The American doesn't think the fees are expensive.

7 Study the notes. Then listen to the conversation again. Listen for the details that you need and complete the notes.

Student loans in Britain

1 Brit students can get loans for _____ and living expenses

2 Interest: _____ %

3 Start paying back when earning
   £ _____ a year

4 Max univ fees: £ _____ a year

PRONUNCIATION: diphthongs

> vowel sound + vowel sound = diphthong.
> For example: /e/ + /ɪ/ = /eɪ/ in _pay_ /peɪ/

8 47 **Listen and repeat.**

/eɪ/	/əʊ/	/eə/
pay	loan	where

9 48 **Listen and write these words under the correct heading in the table in Exercise 8.**

1	boat	4	<u>pa</u>per	7	same
2	<u>care</u>ful	5	<u>pa</u>rents	8	show
3	note	6	safe	9	wear

DICTATION

10 49 **Listen and complete the information about the World Bank.**

What is the World Bank?

The World Bank is an international organisation that lends money to developing countries. _____

_____

_____

_____

_____

_____

_____

_____

_____

KEY LANGUAGE:
asking for and giving opinions

1 [50] Listen and choose the best response, a) or b).

1 a) Well, I suppose it is.
   (b) I think it's a good idea.

2 a) Yes, definitely.
   b) Yes, I agree.

3 a) Well, I'm not sure.
   b) Well, personally, I think they are very important.

4 a) I suppose it isn't.
   b) No, I don't think they should.

5 a) No, they don't.
   b) No, not at all.

6 a) Well, in my opinion, it's not a problem.
   b) Not at all.

7 a) Personally, I think they're a bad idea.
   b) Well, I suppose it is, sometimes.

8 a) No, I don't.
   b) I think it's a good idea. Do you agree?

LANGUAGE NOTE: *that*

that is not necessary after *I think* and *I agree*.
Formal: *We think that it is a good idea.*
Informal: *We think it's a good idea.*

2 Complete each question with two items from the box above it.

about	people should	~~saving money~~
saving money	~~is important~~	Do you think

1 Do you think (that) *saving money* *is important* ?

2 _____ (that)
   _____ save money?

3 What's your opinion _____
   _____?

about	buy a house	buying a house
buying a house	Do you think	is a good idea

4 What's your opinion _____
   _____?

5 Do you think (that) _____
   _____?

6 _____ (that) we should
   _____?

3 Complete the newspaper report with the words in the box.

agree	earning	idea	put
putting	should	sure	~~think~~

NEWS — MONEY

Money or children first?

A recent survey in Britain gives a mixed message to fathers. The survey question was 'Do you ¹ *think* that men should focus on money or their children?'
    The results are different for different age groups. In the 18–34 age group, 37% of people agree that ² _____ money is the most important job for a father but 41% think that children ³ _____ come first and money second. 22% are not ⁴ _____.
    However, in the older 35–54 age group, 47% ⁵ _____ that men should ⁶ _____ their jobs first and their children second. Only 35% think that ⁷ _____ children before work is a good ⁸ _____ for men.
    Most people in the older group were parents. In the younger group, more than half did not have children.

NEWS — 64

PRONUNCIATION:
stressed words

4a Underline the stressed word in B's response.

1 A: Do you think it's a good idea?
   B: Yes. What do you think?

2 A: Do you think it's important?
   B: No. Do you think it's important?

3 A: What's your opinion?
   B: I'm not sure. What's your opinion?

4 A: I think we should save the money.
   B: Well, I think we should spend it.

5 A: Do you think it's a good idea?
   B: No. I think it's a bad idea.

4b [51] Listen and check your answers.

WRITING SKILLS: a formal letter

1 Complete the text about writing a formal letter with the words and phrases in the box.

and	also	as well	but
however	in addition	or	that

When you write a letter, you are the *sender*. When you get a letter, you are the *recipient*.

Informal letters have just the sender's address at the top on the right (but not the sender's name).
¹ *However*, formal letters have the recipient's name and address ²_____ as the sender's address.

The recipient's name and address on the left shows ³_____ the letter is a formal or business letter.

We usually write the date below the sender's address, but it can ⁴_____ go above the recipient's address.

The greeting is *Dear* + the recipient's name. When we don't know the name, we write *Dear Sir/Madam*.

The first paragraph of the letter explains the reason for writing ⁵_____ the main part of the letter comes next. ⁶_____, there is a short final paragraph, which is often about something in the future.

In British English, formal letters end with *Yours sincerely* ⁷_____ *Yours faithfully* ⁸_____, in US English, they end with *Yours truly*. Finally, write the sender's name.

2 Complete these notes about formal letters. Use the information in Exercise 1 to help you.

(Not sender's ¹ *name*)

Sender's ²_____

The ³_____

The recipient's address

Dear + name

or *Dear* ⁴_____ / _____

(Subject reference)

First paragraph: ⁵_____ for writing

⁶_____ part of letter

Last paragraph: often about the future

End:

Yours ⁷_____

(after *Dear* + name)

or *Yours* ⁸_____

(after *Dear Sir/Madam*)

or *Yours* ⁹_____ (in the USA)

¹⁰_____ name

VOCABULARY: words from the lesson

3a Read the clues and complete the puzzle.

1 An interest _____ of 5%

2 The bank offers students a £500 interest-free _____ .

3 The bank has a _____ in every city.

4 I opened an _____ at the bank.

5 Students get a 20% _____ on tickets.

6 The charge was a mistake. Please _____ it.

7 My bank sends me a _____ every month.

8 I lost my phone on holiday but I had travel _____ so I got a new one.

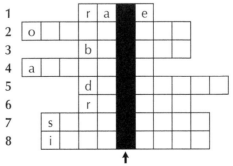

3b What is the mystery word?

11 Homes

11.1 MY HOME, MY CASTLE

READING

1 Complete the text with *right* or *wrong*.

Scientists and other people often tell us about the future. Sometimes their ideas are right but they are often wrong. In the year 1950, one scientist said, 'In 2000, most homes will have a robot. The robot will clean the house and cook meals.' He was ¹_____. In 1955, someone said, 'In the year 2000, every home will have a helicopter.' He was very ²_____! In 1960, another scientist said, 'In 2000, some homes will make electricity from sunlight.' He was ³_____.

LISTENING

2 52 Listen and complete the information. Then decide: were the ideas right (✓) or wrong (✗)?

	Year	Idea about 2000	✓ / ✗
1	1950	Most people will live to _115_	✗
2		Big underground _____ _____	
3		_____ centres outside cities	
4	1965	_____% of people won't get married	
5		A golf course on the _____	
6		_____ in many homes	
7		Computers will _____ _____	

VOCABULARY: compound nouns

3 53 Listen and repeat the compound nouns. (The stress is nearly always on the first noun.)

1 <u>theme</u> park
2 <u>tennis</u> court
3 se<u>cu</u>rity guards
4 <u>Internet</u> café
5 <u>post</u> office
6 po<u>lice</u> station
7 <u>railway</u> station
8 <u>business</u> centre

4 Choose the best word to complete the sentences.

1 The *swim/swimming/swims* pool is closed.
2 There's a gym at the *sport/sporting/sports* centre.
3 Where's the nearest *post/posts/posting* office?
4 My car is in the car *parking/parks/park*.
5 Is there a shoe shop in the *shops/shop/shopping* centre?
6 The house has a big garden with many *play/plays/playing* areas for children.

5 Complete the compound nouns from earlier units with the words in the box.

| card | driver | films | oil |
| room | ~~school~~ | stop | time |

1 You can learn English at a language _school_.
2 Italy produces good olive _____.
3 Do you know the flight's arrival _____?
4 I'll see you at the bus _____.
5 Do you like horror _____?
6 I worked as a taxi _____.
7 Can I pay by credit _____?
8 There are eight chairs in the dining _____.

SPELLING: one word or two?

6 We write some compound nouns as one word. Write the compound nouns correctly. Then check in your dictionary.

1 police + man = _policeman_
2 police + officer = _police officer_
3 book + shop = _____
4 cheque + book = _____
5 class + room = _____
6 clothes + shop = _____
7 fruit + juice = _____
8 note + book = _____
9 time + table = _____
10 wheel + chair = _____

GRAMMAR: *will, won't*

7a Read about Li Chang.

Li Chang is flying to London to learn English at a language school in central London. The flight's arrival time is 5 p.m. London time (= midnight Beijing time). Her accommodation in London is with an English family. The family's house is an hour from the airport and 20 minutes from the language school by bus.

7b Complete the questions and answers with the words in brackets and *will* or *won't*.

1 (she   arrive)
   Q: *Will she arrive* before the school closes at 5 p.m.?
   A: No, *she won't* .

2 (she   get)
   Q: What time _____ to the house?
   A: I think _____ there at about 7 p.m.

3 (it   be)
   Q: What time _____ in Beijing?
   A: _____ 2 a.m.

4 (she   feel)
   Q: How _____ after her long trip.
   A: I think _____ very tired.

5 (she   want)
   Q: _____ to go out and see London?
   A: No, _____. She'll want to sleep.

6 (she   need)
   Q: What help _____ in the morning?
   A: _____ directions to the school.

8 Complete the email which Li Chang received from the language school last week. Use the verbs in the box and *will* or *won't*.

arrive	be	give	have	know
~~meet~~	drive	welcome		

From... Sheila Davies
To... Li Chang
Subject: Arrival information

Dear Ms Chang

Here is some information about your arrival in London. A driver [1] *will meet* you at the airport. You [2]_____ him because he will have a big card with your name on it. He [3]_____ you to your accommodation because the school [4]_____ open at that time. You [5]_____ at the house at about 7 p.m. The name of the family is Worth. Mr and Mrs Worth [6]_____ you and they [7]_____ you a meal. In the morning, you will need to take the bus to the school. You [8]_____ any difficulty because Mr or Mrs Worth will show you the bus stop.

We are looking forward to seeing you at the school.

Best wishes
Sheila Davies
(Accommodation Officer)

DICTATION

9 [54] Listen to the accommodation officer dictating a message. Complete the message.

Dear Mr _____

_____

_____

_____

_____

_____

_____

_____

_____

VOCABULARY: green living

1 Choose the best word to complete the sentences.

1 Switch off the *TV*/*turbine*/*newspaper*.

2 Recycle *lights*/*paper*/*electricity*.

3 *Do*/*Make*/*Have* a shower.

4 Save *sun*/*baths*/*energy*.

5 Use a *lid*/*button*/*panel* to cover a saucepan.

6 Turn off *taps*/*saucepans*/*food*.

7 Use low-energy light *turbines*/*bulbs*/*power*.

8 Use *solar*/*sun*/*wind* panels.

READING

2 Read the article *A greener house*. Say if these sentences are true, false or if the text doesn't say.

1 Green is Hockings' favourite colour.   *doesn't say*

2 He is going to make electricity at home.

3 He is going to get water from the water company.

4 They are going to use waste water in the garden.

5 Many Australian houses are greener than this.

READ BETTER

Notice changes in time focus (present/past/future).

In many texts, the time focus is the same from beginning to end, but in *this* text the time focus changes.

3 Look at the underlined phrases in the text. What is the time focus in the text? Write *past*, *present* or *future*.

1 green living ... more popular   *present*

2 wind turbine on the roof   *future*

3 carry the rainwater ... under the house

4 this area first

5 water companies ... use energy

6 recycle waste water

7 fruit trees

8 one of the greenest town houses

A greener house

Green living is becoming more popular and more people are building green homes. One example is Bernard Hockings from Australia. He is building a three-bedroom town house for his family and he wants to make the house as green as possible.

Bernard Hockings on the site of his eco-friendly house

He plans to use only green electricity. He is going to put a wind turbine on the roof to make electricity from the wind, and he is going to use solar panels to make electricity from the sun.

He is not going to connect his house to the water company. He wants to use a different system. His system will collect rainwater and carry the rainwater to a large area under the house. He made this area first, before he started building, and it will hold 40,000 litres of water.

Water companies supply water to houses through hundreds of kilometres of pipes. This process uses energy and they use more energy taking away the waste water. However, Bernard's family are going to recycle all the waste water from the house. They are going to use this water to grow fruit trees.

When it is finished, the house will be one of the greenest town houses in Australia.

GRAMMAR: *be going to*

4 Which four sentences match the pictures?

| 1 _h_ | 3 _____ |
| 2 _____ | 4 _____ |

a) He is not going to turn right.

b) He is going to turn right.

c) She is going to turn left.

d) She is going to turn right.

e) In the UK, this means, 'I'm going to slow down or stop.'

f) In the UK, this means, 'I'm not going to go.'

g) They are not going to turn left or right.

h) They are not going to go straight on.

5 Choose the correct form, a), b) or c), to complete the sentences.

1 _____ going to buy a wind turbine?
Yes, I am.
a) Are you   b) Do you   c) Is he

2 What _____ going to do?
a) does he   b) is   c) is he

3 I'm not going _____ TV.
a) watch   b) watching   c) to watch

4 They _____ recycle their newspapers.
a) aren't going to   b) not going to   c) aren't going

5 Where _____ going to put the solar panels?
a) will they   b) they're   c) are they

6 Are you going to watch TV?
Yes, _____
a) we're   b) we are   c) we're going

6 Read the plans for a party. Then complete the questions and answers.

> Plans for the party
> Before the party:
> Buy the food – Sami and Sara
> Buy the drinks – Anthony
> Choose the music – Eddie
> Tell people about the party – Annie
> Prepare the food – Elizabeth
> Prepare the room – John, Julie & Emily
> After the party:
> Wash plates and glasses – Tanya & Anthony
> Clean the house – Sami, Sara & Eddie

Q: Who [1] _is going to buy_ the food?

A: [2] _Sara and Sami are_ .

Q: Hi Eddie. [3] _____ the drinks?

A: No, I'm not. Anthony is.

Q: Who [4] _____ music?

A: [5] _____.

Q: [6] _____ the food?

A: Yes, she is.

Q: Is Annie [7] _____ prepare the room?

A: No, [8] _____ prepare the room. She [9] _____ people about the party.

Q: What's going to happen after the party?

A: [10] _____

_____

_____.

TRANSLATION

7 Translate into your language. Notice the differences.

1 I have a plan. I'm going to buy a wind turbine.

_____

2 I think there will be homes on the Moon in 2050.

_____

3 In 2050 you will be 65 years old.

_____

SCENARIO: At an accommodation agency

VOCABULARY: rooms and furniture

1 Complete the web advertisement with the words in the box.

armchair	bathroom	bedroom	cooker
fridge	kitchen	~~living~~	sofas	table

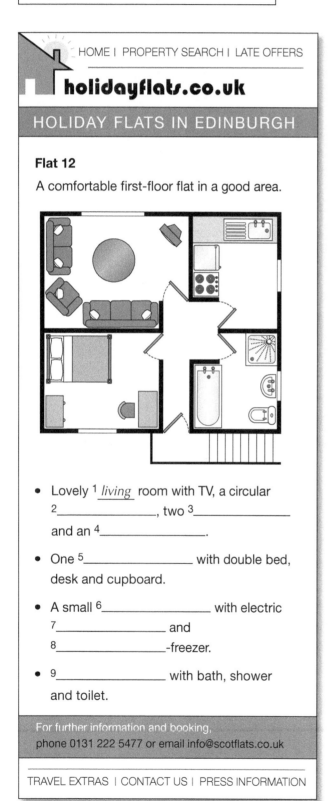

HOME | PROPERTY SEARCH | LATE OFFERS

holidayflats.co.uk

HOLIDAY FLATS IN EDINBURGH

Flat 12

A comfortable first-floor flat in a good area.

- Lovely ¹ *living* room with TV, a circular
  ²_____, two ³_____
  and an ⁴_____.

- One ⁵_____ with double bed,
  desk and cupboard.

- A small ⁶_____ with electric
  ⁷_____ and
  ⁸_____-freezer.

- ⁹_____ with bath, shower
  and toilet.

For further information and booking,
phone 0131 222 5477 or email info@scotflats.co.uk

TRAVEL EXTRAS | CONTACT US | PRESS INFORMATION

KEY LANGUAGE: checking understanding

2a Complete the conversation between Brad and an agent about a holiday flat.

B: Hi. I'm phoning about flat number 12.

A: I'm ¹ *sorry* . Could you ²_____ the number, please?

B: Sure. Number 12.

A: Number 12. Yes, it's in West Road.

B: Sorry. Could you ³_____ again?

A: Sure. It's in West Road. It's very near the centre.

B: ⁴_____ say it is or it isn't near the centre?

A: *It is near the centre*. It's just a few minutes' walk.

B: Good. Is the flat free from the 10th to the 30th of August?

A: ⁵_____ that the 13th
   ⁶_____ the 30th?

B: The 30th.

A: Let's see. No, I'm sorry it's not free after the 23rd.

B: ⁷_____ it's free from the 10th to the 23rd. ⁸_____ right?

A: Yes, that's right.

2b `55` Listen and check your answers.

PRONUNCIATION: stressed words

3 Look at the sentences in *italics* in Exercise 2. Underline the stressed word(s) in those sentences.

WRITING

4 Complete the email about another holiday flat. Use the words in brackets to help you.

To... | info@scotflats.co.uk

Hi. Could you give me some information about flat 19?

(Which floor?) _____

(What furniture?) _____

(Rent?) _____

(Near a bus stop?) _____

(Thanks ... help) _____

STUDY SKILLS: examination skills

1 Choose the best word or phrase, a), b) or c), to complete the advice about examinations.

1 _Do_ some practice tests before the exam.

   a) Do   b) Make   c) Revise

2 _____ start your revision the day before the exam!

   a) No   b) Not   c) Don't

3 _____ is important, too.

   a) Relax   b) Relaxation   c) You relax

4 In the exam, read the questions and _____ carefully.

   a) examinations   b) instructions   c) revisions

5 Plan your time and make _____ that you answer all the questions.

   a) sure   b) check   c) do

6 Work quickly but _____ careless mistakes.

   a) don't do   b) don't make   c) don't

7 Don't _____ too much time on one or two difficult questions.

   a) spend   b) make   c) do

8 _____ your answers at the end.

   a) Write   b) Check   c) Take

VOCABULARY: directions

2 Match 1–10 with a–j to make directions.

1	Take	a)	right / left
2	Turn	b)	the right / the left
3	Park	c)	the traffic lights / the end
4	Get off	d)	the station / the building
5	Come out of	e)	the bus / the train
6	Ask	f)	the bus / the train
7	Go	g)	up the hill / down the hill
8	It's on	h)	your car / your bike
9	It's in	i)	the next street / London
10	It's at	j)	the driver / a policeman

3 Put the words in the right order to make directions. Add a comma (,) and a full stop (.).

1 the bus When the hill you get off walk up

   When you get off the bus, walk up the hill.

2 When the top of the hill turn left you get to

   _____

3 the traffic lights come to turn right When you

   _____

4 come up get to number 47 to the third floor When you

   _____

5 get here When you lunch I'll give you

   _____

WRITING SKILLS: an informal letter

4 Complete the letter with the words in the box.

and	at (×2)	~~dear~~	flat	for	get	hope	
on (×2)	party	so	take	turn	walk	wishes	

1 _Dear_ Rachel

Thank you very much for the 2_____ yesterday. We had a great time 3_____ the food was fantastic. We really like your new 4_____, too.

Our flat is not far away, so I 5_____ you'll come and see us soon. It's really easy to get here.
6_____ the bus to Camden Road.
When you see Camden Town station, 7_____ off the bus and 8_____ down the hill 9_____ about 50 metres. Turn left 10_____ the traffic lights. When you come to the bridge, 11_____ left again.
Go straight 12_____ for about 100 metres and you'll see a big white building 13_____ the end of the road 14_____ your right. Our flat is number 6 on the second floor.

You've got our phone number, 15_____ give us a call.

Best 16_____

Mary and Peter

12 Travel

12.1 CHILDREN OF THE WIND

GRAMMAR: present perfect

1 Look at Kelly's photos and her 'want' list. Complete the questions and answers with the present perfect of the verb in brackets.

Sue and me in the USA

Whales

I want to ...
1 visit China.
2 work abroad after university.
3 photograph lions in Africa.

Sue and me

1 Q: _Has_ Kelly ever _watched_ whales? (watch)

A: _Yes, she has._

2 Q: _____ Kelly and Sue ever _____ the USA? (visit)

A: _____

3 Q: _____ Kelly and Sue ever _____ out of a plane? (jump)

A: _____

4 Q: _____ Kelly ever _____ China? (visit)

A: _____

5 Q: _____ she ever _____ abroad? (work)

A: _____

2 Complete the sentences about Kelly.

1 _She has_ visited the USA _but she hasn't_ visited China.

2 _____ photographed lions but _____ photographed whales.

3 _____ travelled abroad but _____ worked abroad.

3 Answer the questions about *you*.

1 Have you ever lived in a foreign country?

_____

2 Have you visited a lot of places in your country?

_____

3 Have you ever read a newspaper in English?

_____

4 Have you ever written and sent an email in English?

_____

4 Complete the tables about the three main types of past participle.

Past participle ends in -*ed* (= same as the past simple)			
1 live	– _lived_	–	_lived_
2 work	– _____	–	_____
3 play	– _____	–	_____
4 talk	– _____	–	_____
5 try	– _____	–	_____
6 use	– _____	–	_____

Past participle ends in -*t/d/de* (= same as the past simple)		
7 send	– sent	– _sent_
8 feel	– felt	– _____
9 find	– found	– _____
10 sell	– sold	– _____
11 make	– made	– _____
12 cost	– cost	– _____

Past participle different from the past simple

13 drive – drove – _driven_

14 fly – flew – _flown_

15 write – wrote – _____

16 break – broke – _____

17 do – did – _____

18 swim – swam – _____

READING

5 Read the text *Living on the road*. Then write questions with *How many...* for these answers. Use the present perfect.

1 Q: _How many kilometres has he cycled?_

A: More than 550,000.

2 Q: _____

A: More than 190.

3 Q: _____

A: Forty-four.

4 Q: _____

A: Eighteen.

5 Q: _____

A: Nearly 100,000.

6 Q: _____

A: 80,000.

WRITING: joining sentences

6a Read the information in the box.

> 1 You can join two positive sentences with *and*.
> He has cycled more than 550,000 km and
> ~~He has~~ visited more than 190 countries.
> You do not need to repeat *He has*.
>
> 2 You can join two negative sentences with *or*.
> He has not returned to Germany or ~~He has not~~
> had any other home.
> <u>Do not</u> repeat *He has not* after *or*.

6b Use these words + *and* or *or* to write sentences about Heinz.

1 has visited many countries – has met many people

He has visited many countries and met many
people.

2 has not had a home – has not stopped travelling

_____

_____

3 has lost his bike six times – has found it six times

_____

_____

Living on the road

Heinz Stucke, aged 66 from Germany, has no home but he is world-famous. His name has been in the *Guinness Book of Records* many times. He has cycled more than 550,000 kilometres and visited more than 190 countries on his bicycle. He has spent 44 years on the road and has filled 18 passports. In all that time, he has not returned to Germany or had any other home.

He loves meeting and talking to people, so he puts a sign on the back of his old three-speed bicycle. The sign says, 'pedalling around the world'. Many people in many countries have seen the sign and started a conversation by asking, 'Have you really pedalled around the world?'

During his travels he has taken nearly 100,000 photographs. He uses the photographs to make postcards and he sells the postcards. He has also written a fascinating 20-page book and has sold 80,000 copies. He sells his postcards and his little book on the streets when he travels through cities. He also sells pictures and stories to magazines and newspapers.

He will soon be 70 years old but he has no plans to stop cycling.

VOCABULARY:
adjective + noun

1 Rewrite the sentences using the adjectives in the box.

| bare ~~crowded~~ empty |
| lonely pale still warm |

1 The beaches are full of people in summer.

The beaches *are crowded* in summer.

2 The sand is too hot for feet without shoes.

The sand is too hot for *bare* feet.

3 There is nobody on the beaches in winter.

The beaches _____ in winter.

4 On the lake, the water doesn't move.

On the lake, _____.

5 You can feel sad and alone in a crowded city.

You can feel _____ in a crowded city.

6 It's cold here so people's faces don't have much colour.

It's cold here so people have _____.

7 The people are friendly and the weather is not cold.

The people are friendly and _____.

2 Complete the sentences with the words in the box.

| ~~journey~~ travel (×3) trip visit (×2) |

1 It was a difficult *journey* across the desert.

2 We went on a shopping _____ to the city.

3 I love reading _____ books.

4 I'm going to _____ New York.

5 I'd like to _____ around the USA.

6 _____ is good for you.

7 We had a _____ from our cousins last week.

LISTENING

3 `56` Listen to a radio programme about Ellen MacArthur and complete the notes.

1 She is *29* years old.

2 She has sailed _____ kilometres.

3 She broke the world record for the fastest solo time around the world in _____.

4 In _____ days, she sailed _____ kilometres.

5 She has broken _____ other records.

4 Listen again and draw Ellen's route on the map.

LISTEN BETTER

Practise listening to real English radio and TV programmes. To make it easier …
1 first, read the international news in your language.
2 then listen to the news in English (on radio, TV or the Internet).

GRAMMAR:
present perfect and past simple

5 Choose the correct verb form to complete the conversation.

A: [1]*Has/Did/Have* you ever been to China?

B: No, I [2]*haven't/hasn't/didn't*, but my brother [3]*have/has/did*. How about you?

A: I [4]*have been / have gone / was there* for two weeks last year.

B: What time of year [5]*did you go / have you gone / have you been*?

A: In October.

B: [6]*Was/Has/Have* it a business trip or a holiday?

A: Well, I [7]*went / have gone / have been* on business, but then I [8]*take/took/taken* a week's holiday and I [9]*travel / travelled / have travelled* around.

6 Complete the dialogue with the correct form of the verb in brackets.

A: Where [1] *did you go* (you go) last summer?

B: [2]_____ (We go) to Egypt.

A: Oh! Very nice. I know Egypt well.

B: [3]_____ (you be) there many times?

A: [4]_____ (I live) there from 2002 to 2004.

B: Really? Where [5]_____ (you live)?

A: In Cairo.

B: How interesting. [6]_____ (you live) in any other countries?

A: No, but my sister [7]_____ (work) in seven different countries! She's a language teacher.

B: [8]_____ (she ever work) in this country?

A: No, [9]_____ (she not).

TRANSLATION

7 Translate into your language. Notice the differences.

1 How many books has Michael Palin written?

_____

2 When did he write the first book?

_____

3 Have you ever tried to write a book?

_____

4 I have never written a book.

_____

SPELLING:
some problem words

8 Write one or two letters in the gaps to make words.

1 fr_____ndly p_____ple

2 wonderfu_____

3 I went with my fa_____i_____y

4 Yes, defin_____tely.

5 I ate some unus_____l food.

6 We drove a_____ross France.

7 They speak a di_____erent lang_____ge.

DICTATION

9 [57] Listen and write about travel.

Many thousands of people have travelled round the world. Most of them _____

_____

_____

_____

_____

_____

SCENARIO: Around the world

1a Complete the talk about one of the hottest places in the world with the words and phrases in the box.

| also | anyway | in fact | I think | let me see |
| like | so | that's why | ~~well~~ | what else |

¹ _Well_ , the hottest place I've ever been to is Muscat, the capital of Oman. ²_____, it's the hottest capital city in the world. It's not the hottest _place_ in the world, but it is the hottest _capital_.
³_____, I arrived in Muscat in summer in the middle of the night and it was very hot. But the daytime was much hotter. It was about …
⁴_____ … about 45°C. The winter is the best time for a visit, ⁵_____, because it's not too hot then. You can be outside all day, you can go to the beach, swim in the sea and explore the city. You can ⁶_____ visit other towns, ⁷_____ Nizwa and Sur.
⁸_____? You can drive up into the mountains or go camping in the desert. But in summer it's too hot. Most people just stay indoors during the day. ⁹_____ I prefer the winter.
¹⁰_____, that's the hottest place I've ever been to.

1b 〔58〕 Listen and check your answers.

WRITING

2 Write sentences about *you* with these words.

1 hottest place   be to

The hottest place I've ever been to is Dubai.

2 coldest place   be to

_____

3 most interesting place   visit

_____

4 best film   see

_____

5 longest journey   do

_____

6 funniest person   meet

_____

7 worst food   eat

_____

PRONUNCIATION:
British places

3a Can you guess (or do you know) …
1) the stressed syllables in these city names?
2) the correct sounds?

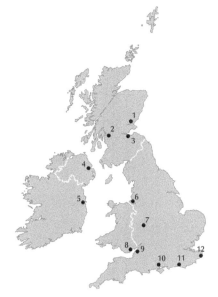

1 Dundee
2 Glasgow
3 Edinburgh
4 Belfast
5 Dublin
6 Liverpool
7 Birmingham
8 Cardiff
9 Bristol
10 Southampton
11 Brighton
12 Dover

3b 〔59〕 Listen and check your answers. Underline the stressed syllables.

1 Read the text about remembering words. Then choose the correct end for line 2, a) or b).

In 1885 a German scientist, Herman Ebbinghaus, produced a graph which is now famous. Line 1 on this graph shows how we learn and forget new words. One hour after learning, we usually remember about 50% and, after 2 days, we remember about 25%. However, we can easily remember more. Line 2 shows what happens when a student revises the words within 24 hours. This time, he/she remembers about 70% of the words after an hour. After two days, he/she can remember nearly 50%. So revision within 24 hours is an easy way to remember more.

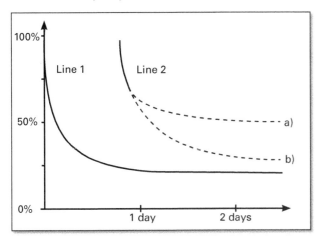

VOCABULARY: adjectives

2 Write the adjectives under the correct heading.

~~awful~~ bad disgusting fantastic good great horrible lovely nice unpleasant terrible wonderful

1 ☺	2 ☺	3 ☹	4 ☹
			awful

We can use *very* with groups 2 and 3, but not with groups 1 and 4.

WRITING SKILLS:
titles and addresses

3 🔲60 Listen to the pronunciation of these titles.

Mr Mrs Miss Ms Dr Prof

Use the titles to complete the table.

	Title	Used for
1	Ms	women
2		men
3		married women
4		unmarried women
5		people with a medical or PhD degree
6		senior members of a university

4 Complete the information about titles for women.

Titles for men are easy – you just write [1] _Mr_ and his name. However, for women you have three choices: *Mrs*, *Miss* or [2]_____. The traditional titles are *Mrs* and *Miss*. People started to use *Ms* in the 1970s and now it has become very common. In business letters, [3]_____ is now the usual title for all women because we often don't know if a woman is married or not, and we don't need to know. For married women, [4]_____ is still very popular. [5]_____ has become old-fashioned but many unmarried women still prefer it. So the rule is: use the title that the woman prefers but use [6]_____ when you don't know. For letters to a married couple, we usually write *Mr* and [7]_____ (not *Ms*). Most other titles, such as [8]_____ (Doctor) and [9]_____ (Professor) are the same for both men and women.

5 🔲61 Listen to the telephone conversation. Write the title, name and address.

AUDIOSCRIPTS

Lesson 1.1 Track 4
1 Is Amsterdam in Poland?
2 Is Amsterdam a capital city?
3 Are Dan and Bob English?
4 Is Ana from England?
5 Is Bob at Manchester University?
6 Is Vancouver in Canada?
7 Is Manchester in Canada?

Lesson 2.1 Track 10
1 Hi. My name's Carly. I live in New York and I work in a tourist information office. It's very busy in the summer. I meet a lot of people and they're from a lot of countries, and I like that. I like working in New York, too.
2 Hi. My name's Melanie and I work in a bookshop. It's a small bookshop in the city of Cambridge. The shop's not very busy, so I read a lot of the books in the shop. I love books, so it's a good job for me.
3 I'm John. My job? Well, I'm a web designer. I work in an office in London. The work's OK but the office is in a bad part of London. It's noisy, the computers are old and, in summer, the office is very hot and it's difficult to work.
4 My name is Alex. I work in a zoo. It's a famous zoo in London. But I don't work with the animals – I'm an accountant. It's a good job and I like the people. Another good thing about the job is the location: the zoo's in a big park in the centre of London. So it's a good place to work.

Lesson 2.3 Track 12
Manager, Abbie
M: City Music store. Good morning.
A: Oh. Hello. I'm a student at the university. My name's Abbie Davies. Can you tell me about the Saturday job, please?
M: The Saturday job. Right. What do you want to know?
A: Well, first, I don't know City Music Store. Where is it?
M: It's in North Street.
A: OK. And ... what are the working hours?
M: Working hours are 9 to 5.30, with a one-hour lunch break.
A: And what is the salary?
M: We pay £6 per hour.
A: £6?
M: Yes. So that's £45 for the day.
A: That's fine. Um... What does the assistant do?
M: Well, basically, the assistant is there to answer questions and to sell DVDs and CDs.
A: Do I need qualifications for this job?
M: You need to know about music.

A: That's fine. I love music. Er... What skills do I need?
M: You need good communication skills. We teach you the other skills.
A: That's great. I'm ... I'm really interested.
M: OK... Can you come to the shop today at 2 p.m.?
A: 2 p.m. Yes, that's fine. Thank you.
M: Good. My name's Mark Peterson. I'm the manager. I'll see you at 2 p.m.

Lesson 3.2 Track 16
Sharks are big dangerous fish. Right? Well, look at these three pictures. You can see that there are different kinds of shark. Some sharks are big but some sharks are very small.

In fact, there are about 400 different kinds of shark. Let's look at three examples.

First, the Great White Shark. This shark has a maximum length of six metres, so it is big. For food, it kills and eats small fish, big fish and sea animals. It is sometimes dangerous to people.

Another common shark is the Whale Shark. This shark has a maximum length of 12 metres, so it is very big. It eats small plants and sea animals. It never eats big fish and it never attacks people. In fact, people often swim with Whale Sharks. This shark is not dangerous.

Now the third example, the Pygmy Shark, is very different from the other two. It is very small, with a maximum length of only 27 centimetres. And most Pygmy Sharks are smaller than this. They eat very small sea animals and plants – and they are not dangerous!

Lesson 4.1 Track 19
Assistant, Customer
Film 1
A: Yes? Can I help you?
C: Er... Do you know this film?
A: Let's have a look. Yes, I do.
C: Is it an action film or what?
A: Yes, it's an action film.
C: What's it about?
A: Well, it's about a man – he's a doctor – and he runs from the police because they think he's a killer.
C: Is it good?
A: Yes, it is. It's very exciting.

Film 2
C: OK. What about this one?
A: Oh, that's a really old film.
C: Is it a love story?
A: Good question! It's a love story, yes, but it's a war film, too.
C: A war film?

A: Well, yes, it's in the second World War. And there are songs in it, too, so it's a musical, too.
C: A love story, a war film and a musical?
A: Yes. It's about an American. He has a café in Casablanca and ...
C: Oh! I know that film! It's very good.
A: It's a wonderful film. The acting is wonderful, too.
C: Yes, I'd like to watch it. I'll take that one.
A: OK.

Lesson 5.1 Track 25
A lot of people think colour is not important. But it *is* important for car companies. Car companies sell their cars in a lot of countries, and different colours are popular in different countries. For example, the number one colour in the USA this year is silver. Second is white, which is very popular. In third place is black. After black, in fourth place, is grey. Then we have brown in fifth place. And sixth is blue.

It's different in the UK. In this country, *blue* is number one! Here blue is more popular than all the other colours! Second is red – again very different from in the USA. Next, at number three is silver. After that we have green at number 4, then white at number 5 and, at number six, black.

Another important question is safety. For example, black cars and brown cars are more difficult to see than other cars; so are black cars more dangerous than other cars? And which cars are easy to see? Some scientists think that silver cars are safer than other cars. Different scientists think white cars are safer. We don't know for sure.

Lesson 6.2 Track 30
This farmer lives in India. His farm is two hours from a big city. He has a large family. He and his wife have four children – three boys and one girl. The girl is 17, and the boys are 19, 22 and 23. They live in the centre of India, so the farm doesn't get much rain most of the year. But there are three wet months in the summer. In July, August and September, there's always some rain. The family doesn't have much money, but they have enough food. In the evenings they watch TV for an hour. They watch it with other families because there is only one TV. The farmer's oldest son is not usually with them. He has a job in the city and comes home at weekends. He helps the family with money.

AUDIOSCRIPTS

Lesson 7.1 Track 34
Assistant, Customer

Conversation 1
A: Hello. Can I help you?
C: No thanks. I'm just looking.
A: OK. That's fine.
C: Hello. ... Oh, Hi. .... I'm in the camera shop. I'm looking at digital cameras. ... Yes. ... OK. See you in five minutes. ... Bye.

Conversation 2
A: Do you need any help?
C: Yes, please. How much are these shoes?
A: They're £80.
C: Can I try them on?
A: Yes, of course.
C: Oh. Excuse me. Just a second. Hello? ... Hi Frank. I'm afraid I can't talk now. I'm trying on some shoes. Can I call you back in five minutes? ... OK. Bye.
I'm sorry about that.
A: No problem.

Conversation 3
C: Excuse me. Can you help me?
A: Yes, of course.
C: I like this jacket, but do you have a larger size?
A: A larger size? ... um ... No, I'm afraid we don't, but I can order it for you.
C: Oh. How long does that take?
A: It usually takes about a week.
C: Ah. No. I need it for the weekend. Thanks.
A: You're welcome.

Lesson 7.4 Track 37
Today, I'd like to tell you about the language of emails. First of all, how to say email addresses, then greetings, then some common opening phrases, and finally some common endings.

First, addresses. All email addresses have two things – the 'at' symbol and a dot or dots. For example, name at hotmail dot com or name at tesco dot com.

Now, greetings. The most common greeting is 'Hi' plus name, for example 'Hi John' or 'Hi Mary'. This is an informal greeting. Another greeting is 'Dear' plus name. That's Dear – capital-d-e-a-r.

There are no rules about opening phrases. You can say what you want. A common opening phrase is: 'How are you?' In the USA, it's more common to say 'How are you doing?'. Or you can open with 'I hope you are well.' An email is often an answer to another email, so you can open with 'Thank you for your message.'

OK. Now, endings. Again, there are a lot of possibilities. For family – parents, sisters, cousins, and so on – you can write 'Love' or 'Love from' plus your name. Women sometimes write 'Love' to their friends, but men don't usually do this. For friends or family you can end with 'Bye for now' or 'See you soon'. A common ending for friends and for informal business emails is 'Best wishes'. Best wishes is very useful – that's 'Best wishes' plus your name. Or you can write 'Regards' – that's capital-r-e-g-a-r-d-s. That's very common, too.

So, now you know. Start sending emails in English!

Lesson 8.1 Track 39
Good morning everyone. Today's lecture is about Roman buildings. I'd like to begin with some basic information about Roman civilisation. Then I want to look at a typical Roman house.

OK. First, when, where and what was Roman civilisation? Well, the beginning of Roman civilisation was in about 500 BC and the end was in 476 AD. So that's a period of about a thousand years.

The main period was from about 50 BC to about 450 AD. For those 500 years, Roman civilisation included southern Europe, North Africa, the eastern Mediterranean and parts of northern Europe. The centre of this civilisation – its capital city – was, of course, Rome.

So what do we mean by Roman civilisation? Well, the Romans were very good at many things. They were good at fighting. They were good at making roads. And they were good at organising things. For example, they organised a fast communication system. This was a system of horses and riders which could carry a message 500 kilometres in 24 hours.

They were also good at building things. So let's move on to our main topic for today.

Lesson 8.3 Track 41
1 Excuse me.
2 I'd like tickets for 14 people. How much is that, please?
3 Is the museum open on Sunday?
4 My friend's in a wheelchair. Could you help us?
5 Hi. I've got two heavy bags, which I don't want to carry round the museum.
6 Thank you very much.
7 Could I have a map, please?
8 Excuse me. Could you tell me where the special exhibition is?
9 Thank you.

Lesson 9.1 Track 42
In 1854, Thomas Edison was 7 years old. He spent a few months at school, but he couldn't follow the lessons because he couldn't hear well. So his mother taught him at home. Edison loved reading and he enjoyed doing scientific experiments.

He started work when he was only 13. His first job, in 1859, was selling newspapers. Then, from 1862, he worked as a telegraph operator. He spent a lot of time reading technical books and, in 1869, he invented a better telegraph printer. He got $40,000 for this invention. He used the money to build a laboratory in 1870. Here he produced more inventions. In 1876, he invented a recording machine. He called it a phonograph. It could record words and music and it made him famous internationally.

His next great invention was an electric light bulb, in 1879. Scientists already knew about electricity but they couldn't make a useful light bulb for houses. In 1881 he started companies to produce lighting systems. After a few years, there was electric light all over the world and Edison was rich and very famous.

Next, he experimented with cameras and, in 1891, he produced some of the first moving pictures. He never stopped working and, by 1915, his laboratories employed 10,000 people. He died in 1931.

Lesson 9.3 Track 44
1 There were cars on the roads in the 1890s, but not many. At that time, cars were expensive and slow. But by the 1920s, cars were more popular, partly because they became cheaper and partly because they were better.
2 Thomas Edison, who lived between 1854 and 1931, is *one* of the most famous inventors. Some inventors are famous for *one* thing but Edison invented a *lot* of things. Also, many of his inventions were important.

Lesson 10.2 Track 46
American, British student
A: Do British students have to pay for university courses? I mean courses in Britain.
B: Well, yes, we have to pay fees but we get a student loan.
A: So you don't have to pay at the beginning of the course?
B: No, that's right. We pay back the loan after the course.
A: And what about money for living expenses, like accommodation, food, books and so on?

B: We can get a student loan for that, too.

A: Do you have to pay interest on the loan?

B: Yes, we have to pay interest at 2.5%.

A: When do you have to pay the money back?

B: After the course. But we don't have to pay until we're earning £15,000 a year. And then we have to start paying it back.

A: That's not bad.

B: Well, it's very expensive. The most expensive universities are £3,000 a year. So, after three or four years, students have big loans.

A: Yes, it's hard. But £3,000 is not expensive for a good university. In the USA it's often more than that.

Lesson 10.3 Track 50

1 What's your opinion about Internet banking?

2 Do you think buying a computer is a good idea?

3 Do you agree that saving money is important for young people?

4 Do you think students should work in term times?

5 Do you think having two credit cards is a good idea?

6 What's you opinion about children having a lot of pocket money?

7 Do you think it's OK to borrow money from friends?

8 What do you think about working in the holidays?

Lesson 11.1 Track 52

Here are some more ideas from the 1950s, 60s and 70s. The first one is about life expectancy. In 1950, one scientist said, 'In the year 2000, most people will live to the age of 115.' A lot of scientists didn't agree with him, but many did.

Also in 1950, someone wrote a book about cities of the future. At that time, there were a lot of cars in cities so he wrote, 'In the year 2000, cities will have big underground car parks.' He also wrote about shopping centres – 'In 2000 there will be shopping centres outside cities.'

In 1965 someone wrote about the future of family life. He said, 'In 2000, 90% of people won't get married.'

In 1969 two Americans walked on the Moon and, in that year, someone said, 'In 2000 there will be a golf course on the Moon.'

At that time, computers were very big and very expensive. People didn't have computers in homes or at school. But,

in 1970, someone said, 'In 2000 there will be computers in many homes.' And, in 1981, someone said, 'In 2000 computers will drive cars.'

Lesson 12.2 Track 56

The English sailor, Ellen MacArthur, is only 29 years old but this young woman has already sailed 400,000 kilometres. That's the same as 10 times round the world! And, on many of her trips, she has sailed alone.

She was alone when she broke the world record for the fastest solo time round the world in 2005. Before that, the record was 72 days but Ellen did it in 71 days. Her route around the world was over 43,000 kilometres. Starting from England, she sailed south towards west Africa and into the South Atlantic Ocean. She then turned east to sail round southern Africa. From there, she sailed through the Southern Ocean between Australia and Antarctica before turning north-east into the Atlantic Ocean again and sailing north-east back to England.

She has broken many other records but her solo round the world record in 2005 is her most famous one.

Lesson 12.4 Track 61

A: Hi. Do you have the address of Mr and Mrs Black?

B: Yes, sure. … Just a moment… Ah, here it is. Mr and Mrs J Black.

A: G or J?

B: J

A: OK.

B: 55 Northumberland Road.

A: Sorry, what road?

B: Northumberland

A: N-O-R-T-H-

B: U-M-B-E-R-L-A-N-D.

A: OK, Northumberland Road.

B: Birmingham.

A: B-I-R- How d'you spell Birmingham?

B: You really don't know how to spell Birmingham?

A: No, I don't. Come on.

B: Your spelling's terrible!

A: I know it is.

B: OK. B-I-R-M-I-N-G-

A: Hold on. B-I-R-M-I-N…

B: G-H-A-M.

A: Thanks.

B: Don't forget the postcode – BH12 4QT

A: 4QT.

B: That's right.

A: OK, thanks a lot.

B: No problem!

NOTES

NOTES